Portfolio Assessment:
A Handbook for Educators

James Barton

and

Angelo Collins,

Editors

Dale Seymour Publications

Also in the Assessment Bookshelf:

Authentic Assessment: A Handbook for Educators
by Diane Hart

Open-ended Questioning: A Handbook for Educators
by Robin Lee Harris Freedman

Managing Editor: Cathy Anderson

Project Editor: Katarina Stenstedt

Production/Manufacturing Manager: Janet Yearian

Production/Manufacturing Coordinator: Mike Nealy

Design Manager: Jeff Kelly

ISBN 0-201-49387-X

Printed in the United States of America

6 7 8 9 10 11   06 05 04 03 02

This product is printed
on recycled paper

1-800-321-3106
www.pearsonlearning.com

Contents

Introduction

This is a book about portfolio assessment written by and for teachers. We have each developed educational portfolios and are currently trying them in our classrooms and respective programs. Some of us have been involved with portfolio development for the past seven years; others have only begun our portfolio explorations during the past school year. Each of us is still learning to use portfolios effectively, and we will do some things differently during the next school year. Although it is clear to us that we don't have all the answers, we have learned some valuable lessons from our experiences. This book is our attempt to pass these lessons on to teachers who are either struggling with portfolios or are interested in portfolio assessment but haven't tried it yet.

Our main goals in preparing this book are to give teachers practical suggestions for creating their own portfolio approaches and to help them avoid some of the dilemmas we've faced and resolved. In short, this book explains how portfolio assessment can become an integral part of classroom instruction rather than just another passing fad or the "same old stuff" in a new package.

Chapter 1 offers a clear design you can use to develop an educational portfolio that meets your own needs and purposes. Chapter 2 describes what students tend to believe initially about portfolios and walks you through essential steps that can support your efforts to make portfolios work for your students. Chapters 3 through 5 share actual cases of portfolios in action across different grade levels and subject areas to offer you experienced reflection about issues you may encounter. Although not all these lessons of experience will apply to your grade level or subject area, each chapter contains ideas that you can adapt to your special circumstances. Chapter 6 is a compendium of portfolio implementation tips that can save you time and trouble in your own teaching situation. Chapter 7 explains how to use your portfolio to assess your own success as an instructor as well as your students' achievements. Chapter 8 summarizes the main lessons of the book in a critical analysis that reemphasizes the practical issues of portfolio development and implementation.

Let us conclude this introduction with a note of encouragement. Many teachers are reluctant to try portfolio assessment because it sounds like so much work. As with any new project, developing a portfolio as an assessment tool for your classroom will take planning and effort. However, each of the teachers who participated in this book feels that the rewards justify the efforts. We believe that if you start with small, organized steps, following the suggestions we offer in this book, you will come to the same conclusion.

James Barton
Angelo Collins

Starting Out:
Designing Your Portfolio

1

James Barton and Angelo Collins first explored the possi-bilities of using portfolio assessment in teacher education while working for the Teacher Assessment Project at Stanford University during late 1980s. Together they devel-oped a portfolio approach that James uses in his Master's in Reading Education Program at the University of Rhode Island and that Angelo uses in her Science Education Program at Vanderbilt University. This approach became a model for the portfolio training that James and Angelo cur-rently offer to schools and universities around the country. This chapter includes information about the origins of edu-cational portfolios, portfolio design, and the payoffs for teachers and students.

In this chapter we share a model for creating a classroom portfolio. We begin by delineating the features that distinguish portfolios from other forms of student assessment. Although the teachers who contributed to this book have different visions of how a portfolio should function, you will find these characteris-tic features readily identifiable in each of their efforts. Next we describe how you can design and develop a portfolio for your classroom.

It is clear from the literature on portfolio assessment that much debate exists as to the "best" format for a portfolio.

Rather than enter into this debate in this chapter, we will share a model of portfolio development that has been greatly influenced by Elbow (1991), Winograd et al. (1991), Bird (1990), and Wiggins (1989). This model has worked for us, and we encourage you to modify it to work for your specific classroom situation.

The chapter concludes with a description of the benefits we see for using portfolios as an assessment tool. These benefits will also be readily apparent in following chapters.

Distinguishing Characteristics of an Education Portfolio

We believe seven characteristics are essential to the development of educational portfolios. First, portfolios are multi-sourced. They offer you an opportunity to evaluate a variety of specific evidence when making determinations about learner competency. Second, they are authentic. Your classroom instruction and the multiple pieces of evidence in the portfolios are directly linked. Third, portfolios are a form of dynamic assessment. They capture growth and change in students over time. In this sense, educational portfolios lie somewhere between art portfolios and finance portfolios. Portfolios in art contain only the artist's self-selected, best work to fit a specific interest or demand. In finance the portfolio is an ongoing record of all financial transactions. In contrast to these two models, the educational portfolio contains self-selected student work at various points in the student's learning rather than a sampling of only the best work.

The fourth characteristic of our portfolio design is explicitness of purpose. You must explicitly define and share the purpose of your instruction so students know what is expected of them before they begin developing their portfolio evidence. This emphasis on clear purpose leads to a fifth characteristic—integration. This means the evidence students compile must establish a correspondence between their academic course work and their life experiences. For example, students learning about the different U.S. states might be asked to compare and contrast the ways their personal lives would be affected by living in a different region of the country. Student ownership is the sixth characteristic of an educational portfolio. Each portfolio is a unique creation because the student determines what evidence to include and completes a self-evaluative reflection as part of the development process. The seventh characteristic of an educational portfolio is its multipurposed nature. You can assess the effectiveness of your instruction using the same evidence you use to evaluate your students. And students' portfolios can be useful beyond a single assignment or course. The portfolios can provide a vital instructional link across grade levels and subject areas when shared with other teachers.

Portfolio Design and Development

Our portfolio design has three closely related but distinct aspects: ***purposes, evidence,*** and ***assessment criteria.*** Purposes are established to determine what the portfolios will be used to describe or measure. Evidence is compiled to create a variety of ways for students to show they have successfully met the purposes. During portfolio development students are guided to create and collect documents, arrange them as evidence, and place them in an appropriate container. Assessment criteria are developed to evaluate the fitness of the match between a portfolio's purposes and the student's evidence.

Purposes

The first and most significant acts of portfolio preparation are the decisions we make about the purposes for the portfolios. Explicit purposes prevent the portfolio from becoming busywork. Portfolios are much more than a compilation of student papers stuffed into a manila folder or a collection of memorabilia pasted into a scrapbook. To qualify for inclusion in a portfolio, each piece of evidence must be created and organized in a compelling manner to demonstrate proficiency or progress toward a purpose.

The need for explicit purposes has instructional implications as well. Using a portfolio approach entails making our goals clear to our students in a context they can understand and then explicitly linking these purposes to our instruction on a daily basis. Implementing a portfolio will be worth your effort even if it does nothing more than help you consistently focus on explaining to your students why they are being asked to learn the material you teach in your classroom.

To develop our purposes for our own portfolios, we started by brainstorming one to five responses to this question: "What is it I really want my students to learn in this course/time period?" We limited ourselves to only five responses to force ourselves to focus on our essential goals. We found that some of our desired purposes were impractical for a variety of reasons (such as lack of existing resources, lack of prerequisite student knowledge, and too much overlap with other areas of study). Next, we prioritized our lists and shared them with several teacher colleagues. Their reactions helped us justify our choices in some instances, reprioritize in others, and occasionally add new purposes to our lists. Finally, we began to think about ways our students could show us they had accomplished these purposes.

Evidence

What kinds of evidence are available to you and to your students that show how the purposes of the portfolios have been met? During the research of the Teacher Assessment Project four classes of evidence emerged: ***artifacts, reproductions, attestations,*** and ***productions*** (Collins, 1991). Artifacts are documents, such as homework and student papers, that are produced during normal academic work in your classroom. Reproductions are documentation of student work outside the classroom, such as special projects or interviews. For example, a transcript of a student's interview with a family member about his or her memories of the moon landing would be an authentic reproduction for a unit on space exploration. Attestations are the documentation you and other teachers generate about the student's academic progress. For example, the observational notes you take during a student's oral presentation (and later share with the student during an individual conference) could be included in the student's portfolio as an attestation of his or her progress in learning to speak before an audience of peers. Productions are documents students prepare just for the portfolios. Productions include three kinds of materials: *goal statements, reflections,* and *captions.*

Goal statements are students' personal interpretations of each of your specific purposes for the portfolios. The process of generating goal statements helps students focus on the most important learning outcomes in your classroom, and it helps students take ownership of their portfolios. How much guidance you'll need to provide in helping your students generate their goal statements depends on the difficulty of your curriculum, the nature of the purposes you have developed, and your ongoing efforts to convey these purposes to your students.

A second type of production is the overall reflective statement students write as they review and organize the evidence in their portfolios. This process generally takes place whenever the portfolio is about to be submitted to you for evaluation. Reflective statements allow your students to summarize the documents in the portfolio and to describe how they have grown as learners.

The third and most important material of the productions is the caption. A caption is a statement attached to each piece of portfolio evidence that describes what it is, why it is evidence, and of what it is evidence. Captions are important because they help portfolio developers articulate their thoughts. The caption helps students become aware of their learning as they share what they can prove they know. Also, student captions help you reconstruct an instructional context for each piece of portfolio evidence, leading to more accurate assessments of your own instructional effectiveness. Captions need not be long or elaborate, but if they are explicit they will give meaning to each piece of evidence.

Who actually decides what to include in the portfolio? Depending on the circumstances, you may prescribe all the evidence or leave some choices to the student. We have found that rich portfolios often result from negotiation and include a combination of teacher-prescribed evidence and evidence students elected to submit. Our students have submitted such varied documentation as notes, drafts, journal and diary entries, drawings, photographs, audiotapes, videotapes, models, and computer disks as evidence. The decision comes down to this: From all the artifacts, reproductions, attestations, and productions that could exist, what particular documents provide necessary and sufficient evidence to demonstrate that the purposes of the portfolio have been met?

How much evidence should be included in a portfolio? One piece of evidence is not sufficient, but every possible document is not necessary. One researcher suggests what he calls the **value-added principle** as a guide for deciding how much evidence to include in a portfolio (Haertel, 1990). The student selects one document that best provides evidence of the purposes of the portfolio. Then the student selects a second piece of evidence and asks, "What will be added to the portfolio if this piece of evidence is included?" When the answer is "nothing," the limit has been reached. Students begin to feel more confidence about the quality of their portfolios after they make the nothing-new-is-added decision about several pieces of evidence.

How should the evidence be presented? This is not just a question of display—a pretty cover and colorful pieces of evidence are no substitutes for substance. Instead, it is a question of guided organization. Your students will need your guidance to consider how their evidence can best be presented to make a compelling argument about their knowledge and skills. You can help by modeling alternatives, such as chronologically or thematically organized frameworks. The efforts students put into organizing their evidence provide yet another learning opportunity as they review and evaluate the quality of their evidence.

Assessment criteria

Our review of the relevant literature suggests no definitive approach for evaluating portfolio materials. Educational portfolios are a relatively new concept, so universally applicable assessment criteria have not been established. In his overview of the key issues in portfolio assessment, Elbow (1991) discusses the ways that decisions about portfolio scoring highlight the tension between validity and reliability. He argues that portfolios are an extremely valid form of assessment because they accurately measure the complex variables that contribute to our students' real abilities, but this same complexity makes it difficult to reach reliable agreement among graders. Elbow states that when we are given the choice of achieving accuracy or maintaining clear standards across our assessments, ". . . it makes most sense to put our chips on validity and allow reliability to suffer."

Although we make every attempt to hold our students to the same set of relative standards in the portfolios we develop, we place our major emphasis on getting an accurate measure of each individual's growth. This emphasis leads to the need for collaboration among teachers in evaluating portfolio evidence. Issues of relative standards are best resolved by negotiating mutual benchmarks for student performance at your school.

Our approach to grading students' portfolios is directly linked to the purposes we establish for them. As Paulson and Paulson (1990) state, "What we see when we evaluate a portfolio is the product of the glasses we wear when we evaluate portfolios." As we look at each piece of evidence, we ask, "Does this evidence meet its intended purpose in a compelling way?" If the answer is yes, we accept the evidence (providing it is appropriately captioned). If we find a piece of evidence less than compelling, we return it to the student along with feedback for its revision. Evidence of a "less than compelling" nature usually falls into one of two categories. First, some entries fail to provide enough evidence of growth; this is usually the case when the student includes too little information in the entry. Second, some entries fail to demonstrate an explicit link between the evidence and the established purposes of the portfolio. This problem often occurs when students include too much general information in the entry. In both instances our guiding question is, "What would I need to see added to this portfolio in order to be convinced that the purposes have been met?" The answers to this question help us provide specific guidance to the student.

Having followed this evaluation process ourselves, we found that grading our students' portfolio entries is no more difficult than grading an essay or a project. In general, the quality of our students' efforts and the accuracy of our assessments about their work depend heavily on how clearly we state our purposes. When we are explicit with our students about what we want, we tend to get it from them. And when we are clear with ourselves about what we're looking for, our professional judgments are adequate to the task of determining the quality of our students' portfolios.

The Benefits of Using a Portfolio in Your Classroom

We believe that adopting a portfolio approach offers significant advantages over other methods of assessment. We hope you will find these advantages compelling.

- Portfolios will give you and your students an ongoing opportunity to communicate about the learning that takes place over time in your classroom.
- Portfolios will enable you to view student work in context. Portfolios provide structure for each piece of evidence they contain. This structure will help you see how each "chunk" of student learning fits into the big picture of your curriculum.
- Portfolios will encourage a shift in ownership of learning onto your students (Winograd et al., 1991). Students will learn how to make decisions about the quality and usefulness of their own work, and these decisions can lead to a strong sense of personal accomplishment.
- Portfolios will help you create a forum for students to communicate their ideas in a supportive environment. These interactions will help your students become more articulate.
- Portfolios will help you become a better instructor. The portfolio process will encourage you to constantly consider what you really want your students to accomplish. It will challenge you to attempt new ways of orchestrating these accomplishments.

Summary

Teaching, learning, reflection, and evaluation are intimately related in the portfolio design we have shared in this chapter. It is designed for realistic teaching situations and is sensitive to the different cultural and instructional contexts you will encounter in this book. Above all, we believe that classroom assessments should encourage students to display their growing strengths rather than simply expose their weaknesses. This encouragement helps students learn what we expect of them, and it helps them gradually become active participants in their own education. The classroom experiences you will find in this book indicate that students of all ages are willing and capable of assuming this ownership.

Preparing Your Students to Deal with Portfolios

2

Suzanne Weiner teaches at the College of Education at the University of Washington in Seattle, Washington. She became interested in portfolio assessment as a means of rethinking and improving the elementary teacher education program at her school. In this chapter, Suzanne reflects on what she learned while introducing portfolios to her teacher-education students. She offers specific suggestions to help students understand and value the portfolio process.

Whether we teach kindergarten, graduate school, or a grade level in between, many of us are interested in and enthusiastic about portfolio assessment. As we recognize the positive influence of the portfolios on teaching, learning, and assessment, we are also learning that the process "requires time, knowledge, commitment, and support if it is to have a positive impact on education" (Valencia and Place, 1994). However, despite our positive feelings and increasing knowledge about the portfolio process, most of us know little about what our students understand about portfolios during the initial stages of implementation.

To help you think about how your students might react to the introduction of portfolios in your classroom, I will first describe how one group of students responded to portfolios during the introductory phase of an assessment system unlike any they had been exposed to in their prior school experiences. Next, I will suggest four instructional strategies you can use to support your students' initial efforts to understand and become comfortable with portfolio assessment.

Introducing My Students to Portfolios

As a teacher in the College of Education at a large, urban university, I recently participated in a reconceptualization of the goals and instructional approach of our Teacher Education Program (TEP). The group of TEP students we used were, at the same time, graduate students participating in a new portfolio process and beginning teachers reflecting on portfolio assessment. Their initial reactions provided a unique, student/teacher view of beginning portfolio use.

The students were completing the first of five quarters in the elementary program. At the heart of their program were four important goals: (1) effective teaching, assessment, and evaluation; (2) meeting the needs of diverse learners; (3) creating a positive learning environment; and (4) professional commitment. These goals represented the essential understandings we wanted the TEP students to learn through their instruction and experiences on campus and in the field. Our students collected evidence of their growth in each of these areas. Evidence included journal entries, course papers, classroom observations, conference notes, and videotapes. The evidence, along with students' reflections on their performance, served as a source of documents and artifacts for the portfolios.

In my program the portfolio is both a product and a process. It is an organized and purposeful collection of documents, artifacts, records of achievement, and reflections. It is also the process of gathering, organizing, and using these documents and experiences to inform learning and instruction.

Getting Student Feedback

To learn about the ways in which our first-quarter TEP students were responding to a new and potentially confusing assessment method, I scheduled two special meetings (called "reflective sessions") for students to talk and write about their personal responses to the portfolio system. During these sessions students chose to remain in a large-group format rather than breaking into smaller discussion groups because, as they said: ". . . maybe we can impart information to one another. We don't know anything."

During our discussions I let the students' responses guide my own comments and questions. However, I selected key assessment concepts and created prompts to provide a focus for our talks. Here are the prompts I generated for my students:

1. Talk about what you know about goals in general and these goals in particular.

2. What do you know about these particular learning goals? Why is that knowledge important to you?

3. What do you think about this "working collection" concept? Can you relate it to something else in your life?

4. Why do you suppose you are being asked to do this kind of reflecting? Does it remind you of anything else you know about or do in other areas of your life?

5. Where does your portfolio fit into all of this? What is it? What's its purpose?

6. Is there anything else you've thought about, wondered, or wanted to know or say about the portfolio system?

I audiotaped, and later transcribed our conversations so I would have an accurate record of the students' responses.

A week later I asked students to do an untimed free-write describing "what makes the most and least sense to you personally this quarter when you think about assessment, evaluation, goals, learning targets, working collections, and portfolios?" Students wrote independently for approximately half an hour.

My goal was to examine and describe students' descriptions of their initial responses to the portfolio system. As I read and reread their responses several times, I noticed a pattern. The responses could be categorized as either (a) feelings about the portfolio process or (b) attempts to construct meaning about the portfolio process. Whereas 13 percent of the students' responses described feelings, the majority of responses, 87 percent, reflected meaning-making.

This student's response describes feelings:

> . . . *seeing the parameters [or goals] in front of me I find very scary and it's really frightening to think that I might not [know enough] and what if I negatively impact some kids?* (Conversation)

A fear of failure, often combined with a sense of being overwhelmed, was the most common feeling expressed by these beginners. Only one student's response reflected more positive feelings. This student recognized the potential of the portfolio process to capture ownership of learning:

> *It makes it so much more our own and when you walk away and when you go into the field I feel like, "Oh I'm gonna have this in me. It's going to be a part of my growth, it's going to be a part of me." It's not an external thing.* (Conversation)

In contrast, an example of a meaning-making response is provided by this student:

> . . . *it wasn't until I went to the classroom last week and saw second- and third-grade students in this natural process of reflecting every Friday on their week, and looking at their goals that they had talked about on Monday, and what they had achieved, and it started to click a little bit. You know that I can learn to make this [reflecting] a*

natural part of my growth as well. Just like they do so
easily as a second grader. (Free-write)

In addition to the major categories of feelings and meaning-making, the students' responses also represented different levels of engagement in, or commitment to, learning about portfolios. I called these levels *not engaged, becoming engaged,* and *engaged.* The type of response that I categorized as not engaged is one that communicates little effort to develop or extend current feelings about or comprehension of portfolio assessment. One example of this type of response is a recitation of assessment "jargon" that lacks personal meaning. Consider this student's rote response:

I can see the connection program goals and learning
targets and working folders have to one another in
defining the overall TEP assessment. (Free-write)

A second example of a not-engaged response is one that conveys a sense of being overwhelmed and, as such, being unable to acquire new knowledge about the portfolio process. I found that most of these responses suggested that the student's feeling of being overwhelmed was directly related to information overload, a lack of time, or both. For example, this student wrote about the rationale for and technical aspects of the portfolio:

[It] could be more productively dealt with in the second
quarter. We had too much going on in the first few weeks
in the program to get a grip on all this. (Free-write)

Another student, referring to class assignments and "brown-bag" reflective sessions, was clearly frustrated:

. . . there is really no time to do this [and] taking up
lunch hours—[this is] a break I really need.

I categorized one-fifth (20 percent) of the students' responses as not engaged.

The responses I categorized as becoming engaged conveyed a purposeful attempt to overcome confusion or lack of comprehension. The following examples are representative of becoming-engaged responses:

"Portfolio" is still a mysterious word at this point. I would like to see a real live portfolio; just get a clear visual image of what the things look like and what they contain. (Conversation)

What exactly is the working folder? Does anyone see it? When, if ever, will anyone see my portfolio? (Free-write)

I am still in the dark on the difference between goals and targets. What's the difference? They seem one in [sic] *the same, or at least highly overlapping.* (Free-write*)*

I thought I had a grasp of what assessment was—but I viewed it as evaluation and there seemed to be some discrepancy between the two in the class discussion last time. So I'm a bit hazy now. (Free-write)

Becoming-engaged responses accounted for nearly a third (31 percent) of the students' total responses.

The third type of response, which I called engaged, expressed a meaningful and personal connection to prior knowledge or experiences. Students who made engaged responses were actively using what they knew in order to evaluate their new feelings and knowledge about the portfolio process. For example, this student made connections to her parenting knowledge to help herself understand the role of reflecting:

. . . when we reflected, what came to my mind is raising children. I am constantly rethinking how I talk to my children, how I discipline or not, how I encourage them or not. It occurred to me that I always ask myself if what I did helped them grow. In other words, I do have some real definite goals, and I have to keep going back to them to see if I'm on the right track. So I guess this should apply to TEP. Whatever I do, I need to reflect to see if I

am on my way to reaching the goal. (Conversation)

Another student used metaphor to make sense of the portfolio:

> *This is a time of tremendous discovery and new aware-*
> *ness for me. The portfolio is making a way to gather and*
> *tie in all the new pieces which I weed through, evaluate,*
> *keep. It is a good way for me to narrow the focus and*
> *not become lost.*

This student's knowledge about his wife's teacher education program illuminated the benefits of the portfolio component in his own program:

> *The practicality of the portfolio is wonderful. My wife has*
> *just finished [her] program and other than expressing*
> *her accomplishment and desires verbally, [she] has no*
> *concrete written evidence of her goals being reached.*

Finally, this student related his own experiences of being instructed in the Teacher Education Program to his new understandings about goals:

> *. . . now that we see these goals, we should see them*
> *modeled [by] the instruction leaders in our program,*
> *because how could we go out and teach if the people*
> *who are telling us these truths don't use them?*

Engaged responses account for nearly half (49 percent) of students' total responses.

The good news is that nearly half of our graduate students were meaningfully engaged in the process of learning and developing feelings about portfolios. However, the bad news is that the other half were not. Therefore, we asked ourselves three questions: How do you encourage not-engaged students to become engaged? How do you assist students who are in the process of becoming engaged? How do you continue to support students who are engaged?

Strategies for Portfolio Implementation

To address these questions, we have developed four instructional strategies that you might find useful as you implement portfolios in your own classroom. The first strategy is to provide your students with frequent opportunities to talk and write about their reactions to the new assessment process. You can respond with appropriate encouragement, assistance, and support when you know what your students are thinking.

Second, help your students make connections. Some of your students may need reassurance that they can experience success in an assessment system that emphasizes *their* responsibility for learning. These students may not understand the direct relationship among your instructional goals, their own learning, and their portfolio entries. Use your imagination and a combination of model entries, overheads, handouts, and role-playing to illustrate these connections. Encourage students to discuss relationships among the various components of your portfolio by helping them draw a picture, chart, or map of the type of portfolio you're introducing to your classroom.

Third, be prepared to put yourself in your pupils' shoes. You may find that parts of your portfolio process are incomprehensible or overwhelming when viewed from their perspective. For example, without adequate vocabulary instruction, important portfolio words and ideas easily become meaningless jargon to students. One way to teach portfolio vocabulary is to ask your students to list (independently or collaboratively) everything they already know about words such as *portfolio, goal,* or *reflection.* Next, after sharing and discussion (during which you will probably learn that, collectively, your students know a great deal about the words you selected), ask them to predict how the words might connect to a school or classroom setting. Following this activity, ask your students to list what else they still need or want to know about the how the words relate to themselves or their classroom. Students who comprehend portfolio vocabulary are better prepared to have positive feelings and to construct meaning about the portfolio process.

Also, encourage students to think about metaphors and analogies related to the portfolio process and its various components. You might invent some of your own, such as, "The portfolio process is like a journey because . . ." and "My working collection is to a garden as my portfolio is to a _____" to get them started. These analogies also make excellent prompts for class conversations or writing activities. You can model this kind of thinking by purposefully talking aloud about your own "focusing" experiences. For example, you might remark, "Wow, I just realized that the way I'm putting my portfolio together reminds me of one of my mom's photo albums. This album starts at the beginning with my baby pictures, continues through my childhood and teenage years, and ends with pictures of me as I am now—an adult. When I think about my portfolio like this—in other words, when I relate it to my mom's picture album—it helps me think about the idea of 'documenting my learning over time' in a new way."

The fourth strategy is to schedule adequate time for your students to complete portfolio activities. There may be times when a portfolio-related activity that seemed reasonable in the planning stages turns out to be considerably more time consuming than planned. When students feel they have not time to complete their work, they feel overwhelmed. By making time, you make a clear statement to your students about the value you place on their portfolios.

Summary

My experience suggests that your students' initial responses to portfolios may vary considerably. Students with little prior experience with portfolios can benefit from direct support from you. Here are five ways you can encourage the learning taking place in your classroom:

- *Provide* frequent invitations for students to respond openly and honestly to your portfolio process.
- *Teach* students the direct relationship between your instructional goals, their learning, and tangible evidence of their learning.
- *Help* students organize their thinking and time.
- *Teach* the vocabulary associated with portfolios, and encourage students to make personal connections between their prior knowledge and experiences and the various components of your portfolio.
- *Schedule* ample time for portfolio activities.

This chapter is a first step in an attempt to understand students' responses to portfolios during the initial stages of implementation. We must continue to listen and respond to our students as they attempt to make sense of the process. Our knowledge about how beginning portfolio users' understandings evolve prepares us to provide the scaffolding our students need to make portfolios their own.

Lessons of Elementary-School Experience

3

Using Social Studies Portfolios in a Kindergarten Classroom

Jennifer Kennedy teaches kindergarten at Forest Lakes Elementary School in Oldsmar, Florida. She has been involved with portfolio assessment for the past four years. Jennifer begins the chapter by relating her experiences guiding her young students in developing their portfolios. She also shares some of her favorite portfolio activities and discusses the future benefits she envisions for her students.

My Introduction to Portfolio Assessment

I have been teaching kindergarten for five years. My role as a kindergarten teacher is to have a positive attitude and to provide successful learning experiences for *each* child. During my second year of teaching I attended an early childhood workshop that motivated me to begin using portfolios with my students. The workshop presented various research and materials and helped me determine that portfolios were a realistic way to assess each child's academic, social, and emotional growth. Worksheets have become outdated tools for professional educators. My portfolios became "quality tools" to measure individual student growth. I discovered I grew with students as I used portfolios to document their growth. I've continued to attend portfolio workshops and to review my instructional techniques to determine ways to improve my portfolio approach.

Guiding My Students in Portfolio Development

I purchased individual pocket folders and colored typing paper to use as "raw materials" and created section dividers on my computer for each subject area. My students' portfolios include a cover sheet explaining the collection of selected learning activities, which include illustrations, writing samples, my written observations, and audiotapes. I also purchased hanging file folders for my students to store their selected best work. I have learned to allow students the opportunity to select this work. I require each student to share the reasoning behind his or her selections. I use these portfolio entries at parent/student conferences to highlight successful learning experiences and send them home with report cards. My students take home their personal world of kindergarten at the end of the school year.

I recommend you plan ahead and outline your expectations for your students' portfolios. You must share your criteria with students. These criteria can then be used to guide students as they create their portfolio entries. Primary students *do* have the ability to make choices about the contents of their portfolios. Making choices helps students find value in their own understanding of what was learned. Give guidance if a student isn't ready to make selections. For example, when I am giving guidance in choosing documentation relating to community workers, I ask questions such as these:

- Which community worker do you like best?
- What have you learned about how this community worker does his or her job?
- What is the reason that this community worker is the one you like best?

These kinds of questions help my students select their best

work from the various drawings, writing samples, art projects, and puppets we create together.

My Favorite Portfolio Activities

Kindergarten students enjoy learning about themselves. A portfolio activity my students enjoy on the first day of school begins by everyone reading the book *In the Mirror* by Joy Cowley. After reading the story, we view and discuss body-feature details by looking in a mirror. Then students write about and illustrate themselves. This document is dated and placed in each student's portfolio. During the year there are other opportunities for the students to illustrate and write about themselves. When they have collected at least three of these documents, each student compares and selects his or her "best" drawing to keep in the portfolio.

Another opportunity for students to learn about themselves begins with this question: "What do you know about people from long ago?" Based on the students' responses (which I record on a chart during our discussion), we begin to determine what they want to learn and how can they find this information. One activity that grew out of our discussions asks students to consider what it was like to travel long ago to discover new lands. Each student is given a ball of clay and a container of water and tries to create a form of transportation that will float across the "world." After hours of fun the vessels are tested upon the waters. Students complete this activity by writing in their journals.

Other artifacts for this portfolio entry are created by asking students to draw what they would look like if they had traveled long ago to discover new lands. Students dictate and illustrate what they have learned from and about people from long ago to complete this portfolio entry. I use all this information to make a class book. Each student has an opportunity to take the class book home to share with family members. At the end of the year, each student has a segment of this activity (his or her page from the class book) to place in the student's own portfolio.

Schoolwide Benefits of Portfolio Use

Portfolios help kindergartners build a successful beginning for future learning and use reasoning strategies. Students are ready to use portfolios in the future when they leave my classroom. Each student's kindergarten portfolio could become a resource that builds throughout the student's education. If portfolio assessment continued throughout my school system, the organizational skills and higher-order thinking that I teach would contribute to these students' "lifelong learning." When my entire community uses the portfolio as a form of quality assessment, students will continue to "buy in" to their own educations long after they leave my kindergarten classroom.

Using Math Portfolios in First, Second, and Third Grade Classrooms

Jeannie Clarkson teaches first, second, and third grade at Buckeye Woodland Elementary School in Cleveland, Ohio. Portfolio assessment is an important part of the learning environment she has worked to create for her students over the past six years. In this chapter Jeannie explains how she has successfully incorporated math portfolios into a relatively inflexible school system. She writes about the difficulties of using portfolios and the benefits she sees for her efforts.

My Classroom Background

I teach in the Cleveland Public Schools, a large urban district of 74,000 students. I have taught first, second, and third grades at the same elementary school for the past eleven years. Our student population is primarily African American. Most of our 550 students live at or below the poverty level. My district is competency-based, with an established number of isolated math and reading skills to be taught at each grade level. Standardized tests are administered several times during the school year, and teachers are expected to have 75 percent of their class master at least 75 percent of the reading and math competencies on the tests. Letter grades are based on district percentiles, and I am required to incorporate the district's standards into my grading system. For example, if one of my first grade students shows great improvement in math but still earns a 74 percent average, district standards require me to give this student a D.

My classroom is not what you'd expect given this academic environment. About six years ago I began to look at students and learning in a different way. Today, my classroom includes a literature-based reading program, a daily writing workshop, a developmental spelling program, and literacy instruction integrated into the content areas in both an inquiry-based science program and a hands-on, manipulative-based math program. Please understand that none of this happened overnight. My classroom has evolved slowly, with lots of fits and starts along the way as I added one or two of these new approaches each year. When I began my portfolio "evolution" I did quite a bit of professional reading and attended workshops, but I felt very alone at my school.

Adopting Portfolios

My experience with portfolios began with writing workshops. I developed a cumulative writing folder that gave me a good sense of a student's progress in writing. Taken on its own, a certain piece of writing might be evaluated as "below average" by my district's standards. However, the same piece could indicate tremendous growth when compared with another sample the student wrote several months previously. I began to incorporate student writing samples as "keynotes" at parent conferences. I used the samples to show parents that learning and growth were occurring, even if the system required me to give their child an unsatisfactory grade. The system didn't accommodate developmental differences in students, but I knew my kids were learning!

I began to expand my use of student work samples into other subject areas, including math. I came to realize I had found a much more honest assessment, because it allowed me to compare a student to himself or herself and not to some artificial standard. As I often say to parents, "You wouldn't expect all children to be exactly four feet tall by a certain age, so how can we expect the rest of their development to be on a fixed timetable?" I started to become more and more interested in assessing my students in ways that the tests couldn't.

I continued to look for ways to keep track of developmental growth in my students and developed a system to collect work samples in every subject at certain intervals during the school year. For the first several years I was disorganized and inconsistent in what I collected, when I collected it, and how I made use of what I collected. Gradually, I gathered all my "kid watching and sample collecting" into a portfolio as I distilled my goals and beliefs into the following portfolio purposes:

1. I want to show a student's growth over time.

2. I want to prove (to myself, the students' parents, and my principal) that significant learning is happening with my teaching methods.

3. I want parents to see and value the progress their children make in my classroom.

4. I want parents to become partners in their child's education.

5. I want to become much more knowledgeable about each of my students by tuning in to his or her individual strengths and weaknesses.

6. I want to continue to value process, not just products. As teachers, don't we emphasize and value the things we choose to assess?

Math Portfolio Components

Currently, each student's math portfolio includes six components: teacher observations, teacher inventories, student records, student projects, student work samples, and student self-evaluations. I keep my observations and inventories in a large binder at my work table for accessibility. The other portfolio components are kept in an expandable file folder located in the center of my classroom. What follows is a description of each portfolio component.

Teacher observations

These are mostly notes to myself about conferences I've had

with students, notes about their math journals, and anecdotal records of students in action during the day. For example, I recorded the following observation after a first grade math lesson: "Bernard is moving about. He's eager to raise his hand and participate orally. He has difficulty explaining his thinking process in counting backward from 23 to 10."

Teacher inventories

I use inventories to measure students' responses to certain tasks throughout the school year. For example, I might give a small group of second graders a number of place-value blocks and ask them to show me 136 several times. I'll keep an inventory of their abilities to show the number, explain their thinking processes to me, understand the value of each place, and say the number correctly. Then I'll repeat this assessment at least twice in the future and compare the results.

Student records

Each student keeps a math journal about the work she or he completes for me. At conference time, it is the students' responsibility to go through their journals and select entries to go into their portfolios. For example, here is one third grader's entry in response to an assignment to tell all about the number 45:
4 dimes and 1 nickel. 9 nickels. 45 pennies. 1 quarter and 4 nickels. 40 + 5 = 45. 4 dimes and 5 pennies. 20 + 25 = 45. 10 + 10 + 10 + 10 + 5 = 45. 23 + 22 = 45. 1 quarter and 2 dimes.

Projects

My students and I might choose to include student research, puppets, written biographies, dioramas, posters, and math diagrams and graphs in their portfolios. For example, one research project began when I asked my second graders to bring in all kinds of containers from home. We labeled each container with a letter. Students made predictions about the capacity of each container and measured each one's volume, using first a liter and then a quart as a guide. Finally, the students chose partners and created a poster about liquid measurement based on their investigations.

Student work samples

I select samples of students' daily work, homework, quizzes, and tests to include in their portfolios. In addition, students pick one of their graded math assignments each week to hang up on the classroom wall and to put in their portfolios.

Student self-evaluations

My students evaluate their progress in math at the end of each marking period. Here are some representative prompts I provide for them:

- Do I like math? Why or why not?
- Is math important? Why or why not?
- What part of math do I enjoy the most?
- What part of math is most difficult for me?
- What is the most important thing I learned this marking period?

I also ask my students to respond informally about recently completed units and cooperative tasks and include some of these responses in their portfolios.

The Benefits of My Portfolio Approach

As I watch my students' portfolios fill up with entries each year, I become more knowledgeable about my students as individual learners (and people). This knowledge helps me effectively reteach difficult math concepts and hone in on particular areas of weakness. After a year or two I knew that portfolios were changing me for the better as a teacher. Portfolios help me consider the value of the work I ask students to perform. If the work isn't important enough to save in their portfolios, I have to ask myself whether it is really necessary for the students to do. I also find that, especially in instances when I become frustrated with a student's lack of progress, I can look back to where they had been and often say, "Wow! Now I don't feel so bad."

My students also benefit from keeping portfolios. Their self-esteem and motivation grow because they get credit for what they know instead of constantly being told what they don't know. My students take ownership of their education as they reflect on their work, select entries for their portfolios, and set future goals for themselves. I note that my students now take responsibility for their learning when they participate in parent-teacher conferences. My students used to always ask me, "Miss Clarkson, why did you give me that grade?" Now they know the answer to this question because they are actively involved in their own assessments.

Portfolios also help parents see themselves as partners in the learning process. Together in conference, we look at their children's portfolios while I comment on the growth I have observed. The parents become more aware of the curriculum and the kinds of work their children do in my class. Gradually, they begin to comment on our progress themselves. The students and I invite parents to our classroom near the end of each school year for "Portfolio Day." The students choose certain entries to display, and the parents help us celebrate a year of learning. Then I send the portfolios home with each family. Parents are becoming strong supporters of my use of portfolios because, as one parent wrote, ". . . his portfolio not only showed me an insight on what he is doing but it gave me an insight on how I could help him."

The Difficulties of My Portfolio Approach

I have come up against four major stumbling blocks over the past several years. These are time constraints, training myself to become an observer, deciding what materials to include in the portfolios, and working in isolation.

My district obligations are the source of many of my time constraints. In addition to all the portfolio data I collect, I must keep a gradebook of percentile scores to justify the letter grades I assign. I try to keep simplifying and prioritizing what I observe and collect so my grading time is kept to a minimum. It can also be difficult and time consuming to translate a student observation or project into a letter grade. My compromise has been to determine a set of descriptors to represent each letter grade before I start evaluating portfolio materials. My bottom line is that portfolios are worth the extra time.

I also find it difficult to step back in my classroom as an observer. I feel compelled to jump in and direct the learning situation when students want my input. I'm still nowhere near where I want to be, but five years of practice has taught me to refine my observation forms to make my data as simple, direct, and as easy to use as possible. I keep my forms accessible and use sticky notes as reminders (for example, "Watch Anetra during self-evaluation time today"). Sometimes I tell students I am "invisible" for the next fifteen minutes and they can't see me or talk to me. The more I can get students actively involved in the task at hand, the more I can observe them with accuracy.

One of my biggest practical challenges has been determining what information to include in the portfolios and how often to collect it. Here I learned by trial and error. Initially, I found I was collecting way too much information and that some of it was not especially valuable to me. So I began asking myself these questions:

- *Why* am I collecting this particular information?

- *Who* will see it?

- *What* will they learn from seeing it?

I keep coming back to these fundamental questions each year as I force myself to make choices about what to continue collecting and what is not worth my time. I suggest giving yourself a three- to five-year period to try out different kinds of entries and management systems. Try to stick to an approach for a year, if possible, and then evaluate. Reflect on what was *meaningful* and *manageable* for your teaching situation.

My biggest obstacle has been a lack of professional support. I hope you can find someone to bounce around ideas with you. Many times I have felt that no one cares that I am putting all this effort into portfolio assessment. I've tackled this problem by hanging on desperately to my beliefs and by seeking out information about portfolios. The current widespread interest in portfolios makes it easier to find books and conference speakers to help you along the way. There have been times in the past six years when I've ignored my students' portfolios for months, but I always come back to them. I remind myself often that learning is a process for me as well as for my students. Like anything else in teaching, I try to keep my portfolio approach true to what I believe and what works for me in my classroom.

Using Language Arts Portfolios in a Fourth-and-Fifth-Grade Classroom

Dorla Long teaches fourth-and-fifth grade at Matunuck Elementary School in Matunuck, Rhode Island. A twenty-year veteran teacher, she adopted portfolios out of a "desperate" need to change the ways her students were evaluated. What follows is her account of the creative ways students can be encouraged to participate fully in learning and evaluation through portfolio activities.

My Classroom Background

I have just completed my twentieth year as an elementary school teacher in a rural beach community along the ocean shore of southern Rhode Island. My class sizes have ranged from 25 to 27 students of varying abilities and needs. At my school we often teach combined grades such as fourth and fifth or second and third together in one class. For the past two years I have been involved in making evaluation more meaningful for my fourth and fifth graders.

My district has made many curricula changes over the last ten years to orient instruction toward developmentally appropriate processes. Our language arts curriculum has been revised to encompass the writing process, trade books, and thematic units. Our math curriculum now supports the use of manipulatives, computers, and thematic units to achieve its specified outcomes. Despite all these instructional changes, we were still using a report card that merely evaluated each subject area with two grades—one to indicate student achievement, the other to indicate student effort. Needless to say, this system did not reflect the instructional changes we have made in recent years. The report card didn't give teachers, students, and parents the necessary information to determine whether we were accomplishing the goals of the new curriculum.

I became involved in portfolios out of desperation! I needed to make my assignments and evaluations more meaningful to students. Over the past twenty years I have checked off lists, given tests, completed report cards, had parent conferences, and felt that the most important person in all this, the student, had very little idea of what he or she had accomplished or needed to improve. I have long felt that students are entitled to know specifically what is required of them and should themselves be able to identify what they need to learn. Our district report card encourages my students to think they are either all good or all bad at a particular subject, but students have strengths and weaknesses in every subject area. I needed a tool to help my students identify these specific strengths and weaknesses.

My entire school ventured into the world of portfolios with gusto at the beginning of the 1992 school year. During this first year I participated in staff development opportunities offered at the state and district levels that guided me in getting started and maintaining my commitment to portfolios. My portfolio efforts addressed my desire to challenge my students to apply their newly acquired strategies. Portfolios provided the kinds of concrete evidence of student learning that I could *use*.

Getting Started

The first thing I did was have a class meeting to discuss our new involvement with portfolios. I told students that this year would be our trial run and we would work together and learn from our successes and mistakes. I explained I would be attending workshops once a month and I would come back to share new ideas with the class. Next, we agreed on a location to store our portfolios.

My students outlined what portfolios meant to them at the conclusion of our discussion. Our class "secretary of the month," Kerri, wrote them down:

Our portfolios should contain:

- some of our best work.
- work we think our parents would like to see.
- work from all different subjects.
- work we like or are proud of.
- work that shows something we have learned.

Our portfolios will be used to

- rate (evaluate) our work for report cards.
- show our teachers and parents what we are doing and have learned.
- set our learning goals for the next quarter.

Our portfolios can include

written work	drawings	dittos
class magazines	models	tapes
dioramas	booklets	videotapes
photographs	interviews	activities
newspaper articles	book reports	projects
special-interest reports	science experiments	

My students responded very positively to the idea that we could collect and analyze their work to see what they had learned. They liked the idea that this work would be in their portfolios for others to view as evidence of their learning. It was a truly collaborative effort.

Revising My Approach to Grading

Our school revised our report card to match the curricula outcomes we were striving to attain by implementing portfolios. Students made an integral contribution to this revision. In our classroom we began with a discussion about what grades meant to the students. They concluded that letter grades neither identified the thinking strategies they were using nor provided information about their future learning goals.

Next I asked my students to circle any word on the current report card they did not understand. We discovered they had circled more than 80 percent of the words! We decided this was unacceptable and our portfolios would use vocabulary they understood or could learn to understand. Then the students and I examined the district's language arts and math outcomes. We devised a report card that summarized these outcomes in vocabulary students understood. It was absolutely amazing to watch nine- and ten-year-olds writing their own report cards. They were as serious about this as any group of professionals. The new report card the class developed to complement our language arts and math portfolios is shown on page 37.

Report Card

LANGUAGE ARTS AND MATH CODES

1 = Most of the time (seldom needs help)
2 = Sometimes (may need help to get started)
3 = Beginning to do (needs help to complete work)
4 = Does not complete work
N/A = Does not apply

LEARNING BEHAVIORS CODE

1 = Most of the time
2 = Sometimes
3 = Not yet

READING
Shows interest in reading _____
Reads aloud easily at level _____
Shows understanding _____
Uses skills to figure out words _____
Follows written directions _____

WRITING
Shows interest in writing _____
Writes for different reasons _____
Writes ideas clearly _____
Improves in using words correctly _____
Uses invented spelling _____
Corrects drafts _____
Spells correctly _____
Uses punctuation and capitalization _____
Shares writing with others _____

SPEAKING AND LISTENING
Speaks clearly _____
Listens to others _____
Asks questions on the topic _____
Participates in discussions _____
Follows spoken directions _____

MATH
Shows interest in math _____
Solves problems _____
Estimates reasonable answers _____
Uses basic operations _____
Identifies patterns and relationships _____

Asks for help when needed _____
Works cooperatively with others _____
Works quietly during work times _____
Completes assigned work _____
Corrects mistakes _____
Keeps work organized _____
Takes care of materials _____
Follows school rules _____
Shows respect to others _____

COMMENTS _____
_____
_____
_____
_____
_____
_____
_____
_____
_____
_____
_____
_____

DAYS ABSENT _____

DAYS TARDY _____

We submitted our report card to our principal and assistant superintendent (who gave their blessings to this project) and sent copies home to parents for their feedback. Most parents responded that they were willing to give it a try, although some parents did respond that they believed traditional grading was better. This latter group preferred that I be solely responsible for grading their children's work.

My students and I began to identify the language arts, math, and study strategies they used to complete their work. Each student kept a copy of the report card in his or her portfolio. They looked through their weekly folders each Friday for work samples that met the report card criteria. Students completed an index card for each entry stating why it was selected and what specific learning outcomes it demonstrated. We compared the information on the index cards to the report card at regular intervals to determine the match between instruction and learning.

I held conferences with students to help them select entries when they had difficulty making choices. I also met with each student frequently to review entries and add other work that I felt belonged in his or her portfolio. Some of the activities that demonstrated their abilities would not "fit" into our portfolios. We addressed this problem by including photographs of these activities along with student descriptions.

At the end of the quarter, my students evaluated themselves using the report card and portfolio evidence. I did the same with a duplicate report card. Then we met and compared our ratings. This activity was very time consuming. It took me a week to meet with all twenty-four students. But it was well worth the effort! I was astounded to find how closely my students and I agreed in our evaluations. In addition, students were able to set goals for the next quarter by identifying their own strengths and weaknesses.

Communicating About Our Portfolios

My students and I made permanent portfolios by laminating pocket folders to send home each quarter with report cards. We laminated a letter to the front of each portfolio inviting parents to write responses to their children's work and bring these responses to parent conferences. I found that this approach helped parents provide me with insights about their children. Also, my students' ability to describe what they had accomplished and what they were going to do next to become better students made parent conferences an absolute pleasure for me. Parents were delighted with the enthusiasm and commitment their children were displaying toward school.

I recommend you hold onto the comments you receive from parents. Some parent responses provided me with insights into how I could improve my portfolio approach. And, the positive feedback I received from parents kept me believing in portfolios. Here are several representative notes from supportive parents:

> *I want to tell you that there is no greater pleasure for us than to have John come home with a report card that he feels so good about and so eager to share its details with us. Your class and this report card has sparked an enthusiasm in him that we only see in him through sports or food! He was so happy about this project and for that reason we are so pleased. I can't imagine the time and energy spent on this report. Thank you.*

> *A wonderful change and very refreshing to have my child's input on her own work. They really have to think about themselves when they evaluate. I'm glad to see the A's, B's, and C's gone but the teacher's perceptions of student effort is still important to me.*

This comment comes from the parent of a special-needs child:

I think it is very helpful for Meg to compare what she feels her performance is with the teacher. This comparison is only useful when the differences are discussed. She is often rating herself higher than the teacher. Specific examples which show this difference should help Meg understand and motivate her to improve. She has become quite a reader at home. Thanks for your efforts.

The following is a student description of our evaluation progress that appeared in our school newspaper:

"Report Cards and Portfolios"
by Kate, Jackie, and Steve
Pencil Box Press
Nov./Dec. 1993

Would you like to know how Mrs. Long's class does report cards? Here's how. . . .

First our teacher passes out self-evaluation sheets. Some of the subjects on these are social studies, reading, math, health, writing, spelling, and science. Then we pick out some work we've done in each subject and write why we picked those activities. Then each kid meets with the teacher. Next we show her our work and discuss what we need to work on.

When every kid is done conferencing with the teacher, she passes out folders with a note to parents on the front. Then the kids take out 3 or 4 things from their portfolios and folders to show parents our best work. We put these in with our student self-assessments and report cards and take them home.

Our parents look at them and, hopefully, they can see our improvements. When they are done, they are supposed to write notes to us about our work. Finally, we bring our showcase folders with the examples and notes back to the teacher.

*My whole class liked it this way because we could see
and understand our report cards. It is understandable
for the kids in the class and our parents. I liked our portfolio conferences. It's a private time when we can talk to
each other. I can tell the teacher what's bothering me. I
like how the teacher doesn't talk to anybody during
when we are conferencing.*

Reflections on My First Year Using Portfolios

My initial portfolio experiences suggest that three things are
crucial to their effectiveness: student involvement, clear evaluation criteria, and collegial support.

Student involvement

Students must be involved in selecting the work that will be
included in their portfolios. This involvement results in positive
student attitudes and responsibility in completing work to the
best of their abilities. My students and I found it essential to
have a regularly scheduled time to select and analyze activities
we wanted to include in our portfolios. Students are more
responsive to instruction when *they* set learning goals for
themselves.

Clear evaluation criteria

Students must know the criteria that is applied to their work for
grading purposes. These criteria focus the students on what
they are doing well and what they need to improve.

Collegial support

Beginning portfolio users need the support of other teachers
who are implementing portfolios in their classrooms. The suggestions I received from other teachers who were wrestling
with the same problems were critical to me when I encountered
difficulties. I might have reverted back to doing evaluation via
the grade book and criteria-referenced tests without this support.

As I reflect on my first year of portfolio activities, I am pleased with the increased commitment to learning I have begun to foster in my students. I have always felt that students need to feel safe, secure, and appreciated for their uniqueness before they take risks to try new ideas. Portfolios put this belief to the test. Next year I begin a new assignment teaching sixth grade. I will have to contend with the traditional report card, but I will continue to incorporate portfolios as a basis for grading my students. The portfolio process allows my students to speak and to be heard in my classroom. And who better to communicate instructional needs and progress than the very ones who are expected to do the job?

Lessons of Middle-School Experience

4

Using Science Portfolios in a Sixth-Grade Classroom

Angie Williams teaches sixth grade at Wakulla Middle
School in Crawfordville, Florida. She began experiment-
ing with portfolio assessment three years ago. In this
chapter, Angie shares the significant strides she has
made in portfolio design and evaluation as a result of
her experiences in helping her students develop their
first portfolios.

My Classroom Background

I am a sixth-grade teacher in the only middle school in a rural
North Florida county. I teach three life-science classes and two
other subjects as a member of a three-teacher interdisciplinary
team. Our team plans together daily, integrating curriculum as
much as possible as we share experiences and discuss ways to
alleviate our students' problems. I feel fortunate to be on a
team that shares compatible teaching styles and philosophies. I
work in a school where teachers are treated as true professionals, innovation and teacher creativity are applauded, and auton-
omy is conferred. Over the years this supportive situation has
made it possible for my team to experiment with many different
motivational approaches, instructional strategies, and assessment techniques. We feel empowered to make the changes we

think will bring improvements when we become dissatisfied with some aspect of our educational program.

Three years ago I decided to have a go at portfolio assessment with my life-science classes. I had recently instituted many instructional changes and was piloting some new and very exciting curriculum materials from the Middle Grades Life Science Curriculum Development Project at Stanford University. I was happy with the wonderful things students were learning and doing in my science classroom, and they all seemed to be enjoying science. However, my grading system remained unchanged and student report cards were very predictable. Students who were motivated to make good grades turned in their assignments and did well on quizzes and tests. Some students yo-yoed between spurts of excellence and sieges of indifference; others consistently worked at an "average" level. Sadly, six to eight of my students never made a passing grade on a single one of my science tests. How could I feel good about that?

I went to my students with some hard questions. Was the material I taught too difficult? Was it not engaging? Was my instruction ineffective? Were my assignments and tests unreasonable? Were they really trying? How much responsibility were they taking for their own learning? My students were quick to reassure me the class was engaging and understandable. Science was enjoyable to them, and they felt they were learning a lot. I began to realize that, although my students had their academic strengths, some of them would never become good test takers. I decided to try portfolio assessment as a means of drawing on my students' strengths.

First Steps: Setting Portfolio Goals

I attended a lecture on portfolio assessment delivered by Dr. Angelo Collins and returned to my school eager to give it a try. The idea of students assembling an individualized collection of evidence to prove they were learning science made perfect sense to me. The evidence could take many forms and would include assigned work, student-initiated projects, and attestations of learning from other individuals. I needed four essential elements to get started. These were

- *learning goals* for each unit we studied,
- *a collection folder* for each student's accumulated work,
- *a receptacle for the evidence* students selected for their portfolios, and
- *lots of sticky notes* for students to use to *caption* their evidence.

The last three elements proved to be the easiest to acquire. I purchased a box of manila file folders to serve as collection folders and a large file box for each science class. I hoped to prevent the loss of potentially important pieces of evidence by keeping all student work in the classroom. I also purchased many, many packs of sticky notes and a pocket folder for each student to serve as the receptacle for evidence.

I was surprised, however, to find that setting learning goals was very difficult. Many of the portfolios Dr. Collins had used as examples during her talk were designed to show mastery of only one learning goal. However, I wanted to specify *several* goals for each unit of science. For my first try I chose a unit on genetics. Never having taught the unit, I wasn't exactly sure what to emphasize with my sixth-grade students. Also, I wasn't sure what kind of goals were appropriate for portfolio assessment. Content objectives are important to me, but I also value other kinds of learning (such as the development of thinking strategies and changes in attitude). I plunged ahead into the genetics unit despite these uncertainties. I told my students they would be collecting all of their work in folders and, at the end of the five-week unit, they would be using the folders to assemble a collection of evidence that showed how much they had learned.

This was certainly not an ideal way to begin. Goals and learning objectives should precede instruction. My subsequent portfolio assignments have begun with the clearly stated learning goals, so evidence can be thoughtfully selected by students. But, as it turned out, my initial approach had a real advantage—students were able to give input into the identification of the learning goals for the unit. My students were very adept at articulating clear and reasonable statements about their learning. They gained a sense of ownership in the process and were more willing to work at this new thing called a "portfolio" because they helped set the purposes for the unit.

Together we identified ten learning goals for this first unit. Some of the goals were specific to genetics, while others were general enough to be incorporated into future units. The general goals created an opportunity for my students to show growth over time. Here is a list of the ten portfolio goals we generated:

- Demonstrate an understanding of vocabulary related to genetics and heredity.
- Demonstrate the ability to construct graphs from collected data.
- Show evidence of family involvement in the study of genetics and heredity.
- Demonstrate how the science of genetics interacts with technology.
- Demonstrate how the science of genetics interacts with society.
- Predict a probable outcome when given a specific genetic makeup.
- Demonstrate knowledge of genetic diseases, causes, and prevention.
- Demonstrate knowledge of the structure and the function of DNA.
- Demonstrate an understanding and appreciation of human diversity.

- Demonstrate an understanding of the processes of meiosis and fertilization.

Matching Evidence with Portfolio Goals

I kept the goals of my first unit posted on the blackboard during our five weeks of study and during the week of class time that I turned over to students for assembling their portfolios. An entire week was a generous allotment, but I needed this amount of time to communicate my expectations as much as students needed the time to work to meet them. Their task was to select work that could be used as evidence for one or more goals, caption the evidence by applying a sticky note with the name of the specific goal(s) it met, and enter the evidence in their portfolio folders. Students sifted through the work they had accumulated, which included concept maps, activity reports, quizzes, tests, tables and graphs, Punnett squares, pedigrees, stories, journal entries, copies of newspaper and magazine articles, and even photos of the DNA models they had created. I encouraged my students to always think in terms of quality work as they selected their evidence. I wanted them to be proud of their finished portfolios.

When students had exhausted all their possibilities and were still missing evidence for some of the unit goals, I explained that "the ball was now in their court." They were free to develop their own personalized evidence, and we discussed the kinds of things they might do. For example, they could draw, write short stories, or redo assignments with modifications. Rather than retake a test, I stipulated that a new test be written and administered to other students. I tried to impress upon students that, even though we had finished formal instruction on the unit, the learning was not yet over. There was still time to succeed if they realized they had not adequately learned something or had no evidence to prove it.

The first two days of the assembly week were the hardest. I

spent the first day explaining what I wanted them to do and fielding questions. The second day brought more specific questions about my criteria for proof of mastery. For example, students wanted to know how many pieces of evidence were necessary to prove mastery of a unit goal. I had trouble explaining that quality was more important than amount. My students were uncomfortable without concrete requirements, but I decided they would develop their own standards for good evidence as they gained more experience with portfolios.

My more passive learners required a great deal of prodding to get them going. "I don't understand" was their favorite plea. I realized the idea of taking responsibility for proving you've learned something was very foreign to most of my students. They had never been asked to do something that required so much thought and reflection on their own learning. I pointed out to them that A's were now within the grasp of everyone; all that was required was the evidence.

By the third day everyone was hard at work, and I began to like what I was seeing. My students were asking good questions to clarify their understandings of genetics, and they were adding creative elements to their portfolios. Best of all they were thinking and self-evaluating as never before!

Day four brought the kind of classroom activity you wish the school principal would walk in and observe. Most of my students were involved in creating pieces of evidence their portfolios lacked. It was extremely rewarding for me to see them completing work that no teacher had assigned—work of their own design!

Day five brought a last-minute scramble to add finishing touches to the portfolios. I passed out evaluation forms and had my students go through their portfolios and evaluate themselves by marking the form in pencil. I explained that my evaluation remarks would be made in ink on the same form. Then the completed portfolios were turned in to me.

Evaluating the Evidence

I thought about evaluation for some time and eventually came up with the idea of rating my students' mastery of each portfolio goal on a scale of 1 to 5. My rating scale included short descriptors to explain what each number meant. Using a 5-point scale for each of the ten goals made a total possible score of 50. I asked for student input in deciding how to assign letter grades. My students were very realistic and reasonable with their suggestions, just as they had been with their own self-evaluations.

I spent most of one weekend reviewing and grading the portfolios. It took an average of eight to ten minutes to grade each portfolio. I seldom grew bored since each one was different. I found that my evaluations were usually closely aligned with the ratings students gave themselves.

Overall, I was somewhat disappointed in the quality of my students' portfolios, but I reminded myself that this was a first attempt. Quite a few of the portfolios were incomplete, and some students failed to turn one in—the same students who always had trouble keeping up with assignments. I was pleased, however, to see that some of my least organized but more creative students had found an opportunity to "show their stuff." It was particularly rewarding for me to see these students excelling.

I was surprised to find that many of my high-achieving students didn't put in the time, effort, or detail required to assemble an A-quality portfolio. These students were used to making straight A's by regurgitating information they memorized, and thinking about how to show what they knew proved to be a big adjustment for them. Portfolios are "equalizers" in this regard. The A's don't come without work—something my less capable students have always understood.

Next Steps: Learning from My Initial Experience

I followed my genetics unit with another five-week unit, this time on the circulatory system. I let my students know we would once again be using portfolios to assess their learning. I also informed my class their six-week report card grades for science would comprise their portfolio grades.

I had my ten learning goals for the unit already established this time around, and I presented them to my students on the first day. Using these goals, the first thing students did was empty their old collection folders of extraneous items. I set aside class time each Friday for students to sort through their folders, caption items to move into the portfolio, and work on self-initiated assignments. I joined them at their tables during this time to question them about their thought processes and encourage them to review each other's work.

I saw some new student behaviors that gave me a great deal of satisfaction during this period. My students were reading the newspaper and listening to news programs more often, hoping to find evidence to satisfy the science, technology, and society portfolio goals. Our class discussions frequently began to center on real-life connections to science, such as recent findings related to heart disease and its prevention. The learning became more personal and meaningful, especially since most students seemed to have at least one family member affected by some kind of cardiovascular problem. Students shared ideas for self-initiated assignments and were far more creative in developing evidence than I had dreamed possible. Their clever and artfully rendered "wanted posters" and "identification cards" of blood cells were among my favorite creations.

I provided only three days of in-class workshop devoted to portfolio assembly when the unit was completed and found it to be a sufficient amount of time. I used the same type of evaluation plan as my first unit, and my students self-evaluated and helped me establish letter grades once again. This set of portfolios ranged from the ridiculous to the sublime, and, just as before, a handful of students failed to turn in anything at all. With their six-week grades riding on it, I badgered and hounded until everyone submitted something I could grade. Portfolio assessment was not proving to be a cure for laziness.

Making Expectations Explicit

I used portfolios during the next school year to assess learning for a combined unit on the cell and genetics unit. Developing one portfolio for a nine-week period was advantageous for the students who put them together and for the teacher who graded them. This time around, I presented each student with a letter explaining portfolios and listing the ten learning goals for the unit.

Here is the explanation that appeared in the student letter:

This semester in science you will be compiling a portfolio that provides evidence of mastery of the learning goals and objectives related to our study of cells and genetics. The portfolio may contain assignments, tests, projects, news articles, summaries of television shows, reports, interviews, artwork, original or published poems or stories, letters, video- and/or audiocassettes, or any other item that illustrates knowledge and understanding. Along with pieces of evidence, your portfolio should also contain

- *a **table of contents** that will serve as a "guide" through the portfolio,*
- *a **sticky note** attached to each piece of evidence explaining why it is included as evidence, and*
- *a **reflection** or conclusion stating personal reactions to the cells and genetic units.*

As a final check of the finished portfolio, ask yourself the following questions:

1. Is my portfolio well organized?

2. Have I included evidence for each and every learning goal?

3. Is the connection between each piece of evidence and the learning goal obvious?

4. Does each piece of evidence in my portfolio make it better?

Although portfolio construction takes time and thought, it also allows for the expression of creativity and individuality. I challenge you to make your portfolio special and unique. I look forward to viewing the finished products.

I also made large signs stating the unit learning goals and posted them above the blackboard so we could refer to them often.

I made changes in my evaluation system as this unit proceeded. Rather than using a 5-point rating scale to show mastery of each goal, I used rubrics from 3 to 0. A 3 meant evidence of mastery of a goal was convincingly provided by multiple artifacts or artifacts of excellent quality. A 2 meant at least one artifact of good quality was offered as evidence of mastery of the goal. A 1 meant the artifact was of poor quality, was unconvincing, or did not clearly apply to the goal. A 0 meant no evidence was present or that the evidence offered was totally unacceptable.

My clear instructions to students and new evaluation scale made my grading system more explicit. Even though this group of students was new to portfolios, everything went smoother and the results were better than the first portfolios of the previous year. My experience made the difference.

Student Benefits

The biggest benefit I see in portfolio assessment is that students learn to take responsibility for their own learning. Portfolios help students develop the ability to assess their own understanding. Students learn to act on their self-assessments by initiating learning activities on their own. These activities can play to their academic strengths, be it writing, drawing, or performing. Additionally, the workshop sessions make excellent settings for productive social interactions. Peer review of portfolio evidence can be very helpful to students, especially as they learn to ask questions about quality to one another. The teacher, by assuming the role of facilitator, can interact with students more informally in these settings.

Too often students are not given the time and opportunity to reflect on assignments and tests, think about the purposes they serve, and consider how effectively their performance meets these purposes. Portfolios offer students a chance to reflect, second chances for learning, continuing opportunities for increasing the quality of their work, and outlets for creativity and imagination.

Teacher Benefits

Establishing clear learning goals provides me with real direction in planning for instruction. I find that I digress less in my instruction and stay more focused on my goals. I am also able to establish and assess goals that are more affective in nature. For example, two of my science-unit goals ask students to "demonstrate an understanding and appreciation of human diversity" and "show evidence of family involvement in the study of the circulatory system."

Perhaps the thing I like best about portfolios is the time I gain for planning, instruction, and interacting with students. I am freed from collecting and grading papers all the time, because I don't look at every piece of work my students complete. With a few exceptions, I evaluate their work only if it winds up being used as evidence in the finished portfolio.

Portfolio Problems

Problems come along with the benefits of portfolios. First, timing is critical if a portfolio is used to determine a report card grade. Not all units of study can be made to fit a portfolio format *and* a conventional marking period.

Second, it is a challenge to get every student to complete and turn in a portfolio. It helps to keep parents and students well informed of due dates, hold workshops periodically throughout the unit, and devote class time to final assembly of the portfolio. It is also important never to make not completing an entry an option. I make sure my students understand that eventually they *must* turn in a portfolio. I've recorded "incompletes" on report cards when I've had to, and then I change the grade when the portfolio is finally submitted.

Third, grading portfolios is time consuming. There is no way around this problem, but it helps to create an evaluation form that manages to communicate important feedback while requiring few written comments. And as I mentioned earlier in this chapter, each portfolio is unique, and so grading is seldom boring.

One of my all-time favorite portfolios was completed by a disorganized but wonderfully creative student. She was very bright and I knew that she was learning a lot, but her grades were poor because routine book assignments and tests did not excite her enough to attract much of her time and effort. Most of her classes provided her little opportunity to create original or distinctive work. The portfolio she turned in for our cell and genetics unit was contained in a box decorated with a DNA molecule. Her actual model was inside, along with a mini tape recorder that included interviews with family members about traits and variations that existed in their family and a lengthy interview with a friend who had cystic fibrosis. Instead of simply sorting through and using artifacts from her science collection folder, the evidence she submitted was all original and self-initiated. Everything was of excellent quality. She had completed a showcase of the best work her teachers saw from her all year. She earned an A in science, the first one she had seen in a while. This student's portfolio proved she was learning all along.

Using Writing Portfolios in a Fifth-and-Sixth-Grade Bilingual Classroom

Rosa Lujan has implemented a writing portfolio over the past four years in her combined fifth-and-sixth-grade classroom at Ysleta Elementary School in El Paso, Texas. In this chapter she describes how the portfolio helped her assess students' academic progress in Spanish as well as in English. Rosa now works as a bilingual specialist for the Ysleta Independent School District in El Paso.

My Classroom Background

Ysleta Elementary School is located about one mile from the United States–Mexican border on the outskirts of El Paso. Most of our students are Mexican American, and most of their families have a low income. My combined fifth-and-sixth-grade classroom is in its fourth year of existence at the school. This class is part of the school's SUNRISE Program (Supplying Unique Nurture for Recent Immigrant Students to Excel.) One particular class of students consisted of about fifteen recent immigrants from Mexico who were nine to twelve years of age. They came to me with prior schooling experiences that varied from the first grade to middle-school levels.

My students were faced with a multitude of challenges (for example, culture shock, language differences, and separation from family) as they entered the American school system for the first time. This group of students had weak writing skills, so one of my primary instructional goals for the year focused on writing. Specifically, I wanted to teach my students different modes of written expression. I also decided to work on writing across the curriculum to help them see connections between writing and the content areas we studied.

Origins of My Approach to Portfolios

I use whole-language techniques and cooperative learning to support learning in my classroom. In the past I've assessed student learning by using teacher observations and journal entries in combination with traditional forms of assessment such as essay questions and weekly individualized tests. About five years ago I participated in Cooperative Integrated Reading and Composition (CIRC), a national research project that encourages cooperative reading and writing activities. The project helped me adapt my instructional strategies to individual learners and support the use of more than one language in my classroom.

As a result of these efforts I began to seek an assessment tool that provided more insights about my teaching and my students' learning. It was especially critical for me to assess my students' progress in Spanish as well as in English. The development of students' native-language abilities is of major concern to me, so I decided to see whether portfolios could meet my needs.

Implementing my portfolio was not an overnight task. It required a considerable investment of time and some risk taking. My portfolio "experiment" took root collaboratively. I began meeting with a group called the Teachers Learning Community to read and discuss articles on portfolio assessment. We each brought samples of student writing to our meetings to practice analyzing writing quality. We each contributed samples we considered to be excellent, average, below average, and difficult to determine, and we presented these samples to one another for reflection and discussion. We also discussed the instructional and curriculum changes we'd need to make to facilitate the process of portfolio assessment. We worked to link our instruction with our assessments by comparing our portfolios in progress and continuing to examine individual student work samples.

My Writing Portfolio

My students' writing portfolios began with a cover page that each student designed on the computer. Each cover page included a title, the date of completion, and a picture of the student. Next came a table of contents, followed by students' responses to two personal reflection questions:

1. What subjects or themes do I like to write about?

2. What are my favorite stories or books?

Students' writing samples were arranged by date, but each student decided how to separate his or her entries. Some samples were organized by topic, others by genre, and others according to the language in which they were written. The last entry was a autobiographical poem written by the student in English.

Reflection is an essential element of the writing portfolio. Students responded to a series of questions about the portfolio process:

1. How did you feel working with your portfolio?

2. What did you find most challenging?

3. What did you enjoy the most? Why?

Students also responded to a series of questions about the contents of their portfolios:

1. What kind of writing did you like the best? Why?

2. What kind of writing would you like to do more of?

3. What kind of writing did you like the least? Why?

4. Which piece of writing was your favorite? Why?

Benefits of This Approach

This approach to portfolio assessment was beneficial to me, to my students, and to their parents. It helped me provide individual attention to my students' strengths and instructional needs. Looking at each student's writing all together in one place helped me gear my writing instruction to a student's growth in English and in Spanish. And I could always come back to their efforts for further study as the writing entries accumulated.

My students benefited from gathering authentic examples of their own progress. They learned to document their own development as writers. Reflecting on this development helped them become metacognitive about using writing strategies. But the most significant benefit came from student ownership of the portfolio. It became his or her own personal story. This story provided protection from bias, the misuse of test results, and the humiliation of tracking. Portfolios are personal, not competitive, and this related well to my students' culture. My students wanted to see their own personal growth rather than be constantly compared to others. They wanted to see themselves as authors.

The portfolios also provided me with the ideal materials to share with parents. Portfolio evidence is more concrete and meaningful than simply talking about letter or numerical grades. Parents received authentic information about their child's strengths and weaknesses as a writer. And parents tend to respond! It does wonders for a student's self-esteem when a parent writes back with comments about or reactions to the portfolio.

Some Concluding Tips

Portfolio assessment is not free from challenges. I discovered it was best to keep the portfolios small and simple as I started out. I suggest beginning with one subject area. Remember you are on a constant journey of learning. Keep reading, keep adapting and adjusting, and keep revising your portfolio approach until you find a system that works for you. Be kind to yourself, especially in the beginning. Avoid getting isolated in your classroom; instead, seek out other teachers who are trying portfolio assessment. Share with others and learn from them. At times I felt unsure, overwhelmed, and frustrated. Believe me, these feelings are normal. Do not give up! The effort is worthwhile when you see the enthusiasm of your students and their pride in their accomplishments.

Lessons of Secondary-School Experience

5

Using Math Portfolios in an Algebra Classroom

Steven Friedlander teaches math at Rickards High School in Tallahassee, Florida. Steven adopted portfolios as an alternative means of assessing his students in an algebra course he created to emphasize math activities and student writing. This chapter includes several of his students' written reflections about the learning that took place in his course.

Getting Involved with Portfolio Assessment

My introduction to portfolios came when a colleague asked me to teach one of my Algebra I courses in an experimental manner. She suggested developing an activity-based course to teach students with hands-on experiences rather than with traditional book work. My high school's student population "demands" a different approach to teaching: 80 percent of our students are from economically disadvantaged backgrounds; 75 percent of our ninth graders take basic math; and most of my Algebra I students are eleventh and twelfth graders.

I knew I would need an alternative method of assessment to go along with this course. In the past I had given notebook quizzes each grading period to assess students in algebra. The notebook quiz consisted of ten questions such as, "What is the answer to number 24 for assignment 3?" and "Define *polynomial.*" This quiz assessed how well a student could organize a notebook, but little else. I needed an instrument that ascertained what students had learned and that measured the growth students made over the grading period.

I had heard of portfolios before I ventured to use them. It was during the 1993–1994 school year. At the beginning of that same school year I had taken a class with fifteen other math teachers from my county. The course was led by a very insightful and progressive instructor, Dr. Elizabeth Jakubowski, who had us research portfolios. After sorting through many ideas, I was ready to design my own math portfolio.

My Portfolio Expectations

I told my students to include in their individual portfolios any three activities we had done during the grading period. Each activity was to be captioned with a specific statement about what the student learned from the activity, what he or she liked and disliked about the activity, and how the information from the activity might be used in the future. I also requested that one "outside" item, with a caption attached, be included in the portfolio. This item could be anything the student chose, as long as it had something to do with math. Possible entries included advertisements, activities from other classes, and pieces of creative writing. In addition I asked students to make tables of contents to organize their portfolios and to write short papers about their likes and dislikes.

I explained that developing a personalized portfolio would help them show the growth they made during the grading period. My students responded creatively to this encouragement. They used color, pictures, graphics, and writing to show what they had learned. Along the way I found that portfolios can be used to assess many things tests don't cover, such as the depth of a student's understanding.

The process of captioning entries was an especially powerful learning experience. My students used the captions to critique themselves by describing their own strengths and weaknesses. The captions also allowed students to revisit topics and write about them. Some of the best portfolios were created by students who usually struggled the most in math classes.

Grading My Students' Portfolios

Grading portfolios takes time, and a lot of it. I considered having students turn in smaller portfolios twice during each six-week grading period. However, because I wanted to have some semblance of a personal life, I chose to grade the portfolios only once every six weeks. It was important to make the due date early enough to grade each portfolio effectively before the end of the grading period. My portfolio approach did require more time and effort than my traditional notebook approach had in the past.

The first thing I looked for when I graded a portfolio was whether the student satisfied each of my requirements. Anything missing from the portfolio reduced the student's grade. It was difficult to grade for creativity (or lack thereof), but I did evaluate the specificity of students' captions and overall portfolio organization. I allowed my students to set up their portfolios as they chose, but they had to display a clear structure. I also graded for grammar, spelling, and neatness.

I organized my students' completed portfolios into three categories: *outstanding, pretty good,* and *ugh.* The *outstanding* portfolios met all my requirements and showed originality, creativity, effort, organization, and neatness. *Pretty good* portfolios met all the requirements but lacked one of the other critical elements. *Ugh* portfolios failed to meet one or more of the basic requirements. I rank-ordered the portfolios within each category, which occasionally led me to switch a portfolio from one category to another. *Outstanding* portfolios received A and B grades, *pretty good* ones received B and C grades, and the *ughs* received D and F grades.

For the future I'm considering a slightly different scoring rubric (Ott, 1993) to grade student portfolios. This grading system classifies products as superior (complete work, goes beyond requirements), satisfactory with minor flaws (complete work, some errors), nearly satisfactory with serious flaws (almost complete work), and unsatisfactory (work is unacceptable).

The Benefits of My Portfolio Approach

I found two major rewards for trying portfolios in my classroom. First, the portfolios helped my students integrate math with the other subjects they study in high school. Second, the portfolios encouraged student creativity in my math classroom.

Portfolios can link concepts from several subject areas in stimulating ways. I believe that one of my functions as a teacher is to remove the isolation from my one subject area. For example, during a water-balloon launch experiment, each student wrote a paper recounting the procedure for the experiment and what he or she had learned from the results. They learned an amazing amount of physics in the process, showing how effective a portfolio can be in linking writing, science, and math. Portfolios help students function in the real world of making connections.

During the last grading period of the year, I asked each of my students to write a short paper reflecting on the experimental course and my method of evaluation. Two of these papers, authored by LaShunda White and Kristi Hackbarth, are presented in their original forms at the conclusion of this chapter. LaShunda's response displays how students in my class learned to take ownership of the activities and concepts they learned. Kristi's response indicates her understanding of the instructional changes she encountered in my class and her corresponding shift in attitude about math. Both student responses also show

how my new assessment approach directly influenced the instruction I offered in the course.

Future Portfolio Plans

I plan to extend my use of portfolios to my other math courses. My Basic Math students can construct portfolios that help them improve as readers and writers as well as relate math to their lives. My Algebra II Honors students can construct portfolios to assist them in college admission or job hunting. The experience of putting a portfolio together in high school can be rewarding for all my students. Portfolios encourage students to think of creative ways to share what they are learning. They also allow students to express themselves in a comfortable way. Shouldn't all students have the experience of making a portfolio?

Student Reflections on My Course and Portfolio Approach

To start things off, I'll talk about my experiences in Algebra I. First of all, this class was very different. We did things that the other classes didn't do. One thing that we did was the launching of the water balloons. I enjoyed that a lot even though it was hot outside. I liked a lot of other activities that we did throughout the year. Another activity that I liked was when we went outside and had to find something around school to measure. That was fun, too, because I liked when we weren't in class so much. Another one of my favorite activities inside the class was the Linear Functions activity. I wasn't too crazy about it but it was still one of the more easier assignments that we had to do. I really under-stood that. Two more of my favorite assignments were the Birthday activity—where we had to keep adding and subtracting numbers until we came up with our birthday (or whatever)—and the activity with the Picture Solving worksheet, when we figured out the word(s) by looking at the picture. I had seen and heard about similar activities like those but I had never done them. There were many more that I liked, but those were just a few. There were also some assignments during the year that I didn't like. One thing that I didn't like, that I generally hated, was graphing. I think graphing is too long and boring. It's just too much work and takes up too much time and graph paper. Anyway, enough about graphing. Another activity that I didn't like was Systems of Equations. I didn't like the problems in general. Another activity was recently when we had to do Algebraic Expressions. Some of it was easier than the rest of it. Then again, some of it was very difficult and I did not like doing those assignments. There was something else that I didn't like at the beginning of the year and that was working in groups. I guess I probably didn't like that because I didn't know many people in the class. I only knew a few. Most times I like doing my own work. That was probably another reason why I didn't like working in groups. But later on in the year, after I had known more people in the class, it was OK and beginning to be fun. Also, I didn't mind working in groups because the work got harder as the year progressed and I needed some extra help at times. One advantage from working in groups was at test time. On some test days, we got to work in groups and that's something that you're not usually allowed to do in other classes. I really liked that because it seemed more like a class assignment instead of a test. Plus, there was a better chance of getting a good grade if you had a partner or two to help you. With all the work that we had during the school year, I did learn a lot of new things that I didn't know before. The things that were the most new to me were the formu-

las. For example, the Quadratic Formula. I thought that at first, I wasn't going to be able to solve a formula like that. Then, after I knew how to work it out, it wasn't as bad as I thought.

I was glad to be in Algebra I at the beginning of the year. After the first couple of months though, I thought that I would hate this course. But in the long run, I decided that I did like it. I don't have any suggestions for the class, Mr. Friedlander. You just keep being a good teacher and take care. C-ya!

—LaShunda White

Let me start by saying this class has been different than any other math class I've been in. For the first time since I don't know when, I've actually liked coming to math. I liked working in groups instead of by myself, it made it more interesting. If I wasn't sure of how to do something I had someone in my group to explain it to me. I also liked that you explained the homework and the work that we were going to do that day. To be honest this isn't the first time I've been in Algebra. Last year I started out in Algebra I, but I ended up back in Pre algebra. I realized that I didn't do good in Algebra the first time because of the teacher. He explained things too fast, didn't give us a chance to ask questions, and since he had two jobs he didn't have time to give us extra help. I liked the way you let us go up to the board and do the problems instead of you just doing them and assuming we understood. I also enjoyed doing the portfolios instead of semester exams. They showed me how math was used in the real world. I also appreciated the fact that you stayed after school to help when there was something I didn't understand. As I said I appreciated that you stayed after school to help, but you always seemed

*like you were trying to rush to get somewhere. Also when
someone asked a question you seemed to get impatient if
they didn't get it the first time you tried to explain it. I
liked the calculators that we got to use. They helped
extremely when we used them. There are two assignments that really stand out in my mind, the Teeny Bop's
package and the water-balloon launches. I especially
liked launching the water balloons. It was nice to see a
teacher actually get involved in a project instead of just
sitting behind their desk. I think another reason I liked
this class is because we didn't have a book. Finally let me
thank you for getting me interested in math again.*

—Kristi Hackbarth

Using Science Portfolios in a Tenth-Grade Chemistry Classroom

Susan Butler teaches science at Rutherford High School in Panama City, Florida. Her chapter provides a powerful example of the ways that portfolio assessment can influence and support instructional change. This is Susan's story of how she transformed her classroom from a source of frustration to a place of learning.

Getting Involved with Portfolios

I had become increasingly frustrated with my profession after teaching for nine years. Student inattention and apathy seemed to be on the upswing, while my own effectiveness as a teacher was on a downswing. Grading tests had become an especially tortuous activity for me. My students could not answer simple comprehension questions and would not even attempt analysis, synthesis, or evaluation questions. Something was very wrong in my classroom.

I distanced myself from my students by laying the blame on them as I became more frustrated. "If they would only study, listen, take notes, and so on," I rationalized, "then they would learn." This type of thinking made my classroom a battlefield where I was determined to cram knowledge down my students' throats whether they wanted it or not! I had created a terrible climate for learning and, at this very low point, I seriously considered leaving the teaching profession.

At this pivotal time, I was introduced to the constructivist epistemology of Tobin, Kahle, and Fraser (1990). Constructivism gave me a new perspective on my teaching. I learned that my students had to be actively involved in the process for learning to occur. They could not just sit and listen to me lecture all day. I began to search for new teaching strategies that would actively involve students.

My search led me to portfolio assessment. I began to review my instructional problems to determine whether using portfolios could help me overcome them. After some reflection I identified four main problems:

1. I was running a teacher-centered classroom instead of involving my students in their own learning.

2. My lecturing was ineffective in promoting students' understanding of concepts and higher-level thinking strategies.

3. My grading methods focused students' attention on learning only those concepts that could be measured on a pencil-and-paper test.

4. My students did not find my classroom climate conducive to learning.

I set out to design a portfolio program that would address these particular problems in my Honors Chemistry classes. The typical Honors Chemistry student is a tenth grader who has previously completed our Biology I course graduation requirement. These students number between 87 and 97 from year to year, distributed fairly evenly in four different class sections. Girls slightly outnumber boys, and the students' ethnicities tend to mirror the percentages found in our school population (67 percent Caucasian, 26 percent African American, 6 percent Asian, and 2 percent Latino).

My Portfolio Design

I introduced the concept of portfolios to my chemistry students in August of 1993. I began by eliciting student opinions as to why their future prospective employers might want to see a portfolio. The answers I received were about skill assessment. ("They'll want to know if we're any good!" is how my student Farley put it.) Next we compared portfolios to resumes. Students concluded that resumes were lists of achievements, whereas portfolios showed "what you can really do," according to a student named Linda.

I used Linda's definition to explain my rationale for requiring a portfolio in the course. Then I distributed the following handout:

To pass Chemistry I Honors, you must maintain a satis-factory portfolio. An excellent portfolio can be used to raise your grade average five numerical points.

A portfolio is a container of documents that provides evidence of your learning. Every nine weeks you will be given a list of learning activities that you must document in your portfolio. Documentation of 94 percent or above constitutes an excellent rating. Documentation of 75 percent to 93 percent generally constitutes a satisfactory portfolio. SPECIAL NOTE: A PORTFOLIO THAT DOCUMENTS LESS THAN 94 PERCENT OF THE LEARNING ACTIVITIES MAY STILL BE ELIGIBLE FOR AN EXCELLENT RATING IF GREAT CREATIVITY, VERSATILITY, AND ORGANIZATIONAL SKILLS ARE EXHIBITED.

In addition to the above documentation, your portfolio must contain at least one journal entry for each week. The required length for each entry is one-half page or longer. Failure to keep a current journal of proper length will result in an unsatisfactory rating for the portfolio.

One of my primary sources for developing this handout was an article titled "Portfolios: Questions for Design" (Collins, 1992). The first portion of the portfolio was based on the Florida Department of Education Course Student Performance Standards (Florida Department of Education, 1991). I distributed these standards evenly into four Learning Activity sheets for students. Students were given one Learning Activity sheet for each of our four nine-week grading periods. The sheets were used as a basis for student proofs. Proofs constituted documentation that the knowledge described in the Learning Activity had actually been achieved by the student.

My students chose their own documentation, marked the pieces of evidence they selected with the appropriate number from the Learning Activity sheet, and placed them in their portfolios as a "proofs" of learning. I made my assessment in each case by deciding whether the student had included sufficient supporting evidence to confirm that he or she had actually learned the assigned material.

The second sections of students' portfolios consisted of journal entries. Sometimes my students chose the subject of their journal entries, and sometimes I selected a topic for them. We used the journals to give students a place to record their thoughts about chemistry class, reflect on their personal learning, and make comments to me. I based my assessment of the journal entries on their lengths and responded in writing to the comments students directed to me. This practice opened the door for other kinds of productive dialogue between the students and me.

Here are the questions students asked most frequently (and my responses to them) about the process of constructing a portfolio:

Should I only keep my best papers in my portfolio?

Not necessarily. The portfolio documents learning. You might consider having two papers to document one activity—the second paper showing an improvement over the first.

What kinds of evidence will be accepted as documentation?

Worksheets, review sheets, tests, lab reports, outlines, homework, photographs, tapes, videotapes, and so on. The options are limited only by your imagination.

Can I use a collaborative effort as evidence?

Yes. Many labs will be collaborative. Each person may use the lab write-up in his or her portfolio.

How much evidence should I include?

Don't go for overkill! At least one piece of evidence is necessary to document each learning activity. Please limit yourself to no more than three. If you wish, you may add a "Miscellaneous" section to your portfolio to display items that do not fit as evidence elsewhere.

Can one piece of evidence be used to document more than one learning activity?

Yes, but it should be clearly captioned. An explanation of how it is being used for each purpose should be included.

How should I organize my portfolio?

The best way is to arrange your evidence in the same order as the list of learning activities I've provided for you. Each piece of evidence should be clearly marked, and a short explanation should be included describing how this entry shows that learning has occurred. I will not organize your portfolio for you. If items are out of order or not clearly marked, you will receive a rating of unsatisfactory.

How often will you assess my portfolio?

Once a week.

Grading the Portfolios

I created a weekly assessment form to communicate the grades assigned to each student's portfolio entries. Students received an E for excellent if they successfully completed all assigned proofs for the week, wrote a journal entry of sufficient length, and demonstrated excellence in creativity, versatility, organization, or motivation. For example, my student Juan used a series of drawings to explain the effect of changing the container volume of an enclosed gas. He received an E because his illustrations so powerfully embellished his words.

Students received an S for satisfactory if they completed all proofs and wrote journal entries of the appropriate length. Students received a U for unsatisfactory if their proofs or journal entries were incomplete, missing, or tardy. (A few of my students received quite a few U ratings for consistently disregarding due dates.) I also assigned zeros for the week if no new work was done or if the portfolio was not submitted to me.

Students who went beyond my weekly requirements received a comment from me detailing the extra effort they had put forth. I also offered written suggestions when journal entries were missing or incomplete or if students' proofs were inaccurate. Students even received written comments from me if they failed to submit their work. I wanted to be sure they understood why they had failed.

At the end of each nine-week period, I made an overall assessment of each portfolio and a rated it excellent, satisfactory, or unsatisfactory. If a student had not earned a majority of E ratings on the weekly assignments, my assessment plan described ways to get an overall excellent rating on the portfolio for the nine weeks. These alternatives offered more opportunities for students to excel and gave me some flexibility in grading. This approach proved to be very useful in helping my students improve their portfolios.

The Benefits of My Portfolio Approach

Enhanced communication

The first (and most important) benefit of implementing portfolios was better one-on-one communication between the students and me. The majority of our enhanced communications fell into three categories: students' academic concerns, students' personal concerns, and my concerns. Here are some examples of each:

Students' Academic Concerns

"Help! I'm confused on acids and bases."

"How can I bring my grades up?"

Students' Personal Concerns

"Pray that things get better for me. I've been accepted at the University of Florida. Now all I need is money. I will be the first female in my entire family to have graduated from high school and the first to ever go to college. I'm broke and my mother doesn't even have bill money. So, I don't know how I'm going to pay, but the Lord will help me in some way."

Teacher's Concerns

"I used Dale's journal to discuss his behavior in class. He has been very disruptive lately, and I'm trying to get him to think before he opens his mouth. I like being able to do this in private, in writing. I have found this to be an effective method that changes behavior without disrupting class or humiliating the student." (from my journal)

Our portfolio communications helped me receive a well-rounded picture of my students. I was becoming more apt to view them as individuals, not just "pupil units." An increase in class participation accompanied this perspective shift. My students also felt the portfolio was a useful tool in communicating with me. Christine sums up these feelings:

I think that it [the portfolio] is good and it is a real good way to communicate with you. I know without the portfolio some of my questions would not be answered.

Student awareness

Students developed an awareness of their own learning styles and personal preferences in my classroom while using portfolios. Students' journals displayed this awareness:

I suppose the best way I've learned in the past is by

listening. Demonstrations of the work also help, but it's listening that really helps me. I used to always be ahead of the other children when I was younger because I can pick up on things fast. (Pasqual)

I hate walking into a room and seeing every single chair placed neatly in vertical rows. It suggests too much discipline, like we are in the military. It's also boring. I would like to walk in and see the desks arranged in a big circle and maybe the teacher's desk in the middle. Basically, what I'm getting at is I like change. Teachers have been using the same teaching methods and class setups for years: chalkboards, assigned seats, boring seat work, complicated lectures, and crowded classes. New alternatives to some of these things would make the class better. (April)

Such student comments allowed me to assess the needs and wants of my students. I also learned more about how my students learned, and this information helped me become a more effective teacher. Specifically, I used what I learned from my students in lesson planning and adapting my teaching style to meet their needs.

Developing thinking strategies

Portfolios helped my students develop higher-order thinking strategies such as analysis, synthesis, and evaluation. The proof or documentation portion of the portfolio was instrumental in helping students grow in this area. One student's comment is included here to demonstrate the students' appreciation of this portion of the portfolio. Then two actual proofs are quoted. The first of these demonstrates analysis and the second, evaluation.

We realize our strengths and weaknesses and [by doing proofs] we got extra practice for our strengths and when we recognized our weaknesses, we were able to work on them. (Connie)

A physical property is a quality of a substance that can be observed or measured without changing the substance's chemical composition. A physical change is water turning to ice or water becoming vapor. Another example is gallium melting. A chemical property is the ability of a substance to undergo chemical reactions and to form new substances. A chemical change is when you combine iron and sulfur by heating, they chemically change. (Analysis by Don)

We get energy from different things like food, heat, wind, and water. Some sources are fire, water, and wind. Some advantages to fire are that it keeps us warm and can be used to cook with. Some disadvantages are that it can cause destruction if used wrong. Some advantages to water are that we need it to live, use it to cook with, and that it doesn't pollute. A disadvantage is that not everybody lives near water. An advantage of wind is it provides us with electricity when it passes through a windmill. But strong winds, in tornadoes and hurricanes, can be destructive and destroy the windmill. Also, the wind might not blow every day. (Evaluation by Juan)

Meaningful tests

I was able to change my approach to test construction because my students were explaining concepts and not just memorizing them. I switched from multiple choice "comprehension checks" to tests that included short-answer and essay questions. This change occurred without an accompanying drop in test scores. Therefore, I felt more confident that my teaching was actually being constructed into knowledge by students.

Impediments to Portfolio Assessment

Was the entire project unequivocally a complete success with all students? Of course not! I conclude this chapter by discussing a few of the difficulties I encountered during the process of the portfolio implementation.

I struggled with finding the time to review and grade my students' portfolios. I eventually settled into a routine of reading a certain number of portfolio entries before leaving school each day. I never got behind, so this helped prevent some stress. My students and I also needed an occasional "portfolio vacation." I did not require students to turn in portfolios during short holiday weeks and during the last week of each grading period. This gave them a breather, and it gave me some extra time for planning. I used the extra planning time to review our progress and implement changes in my procedures.

I also had to struggle to stay objective as I viewed my students' work. This struggle was especially pronounced when I read journal entries that were highly critical of my teaching methods. I always tried to accept student opinion and use it to examine my practices for possible adaptations. This was difficult, but it was worthwhile to have my students' perspectives about my teaching.

Some of my students simply refused to participate in the plan. I had one student whose failure in the course was due *only* to the fact that he refused to keep a portfolio. I did everything I could to prevent this, including calling his parents in for conferences. I labored to make my portfolio requirements very clear, but I had to accept that this method of assessment wasn't successful with all of my students.

My other recurring problems revolved around the quality of certain students' work. Sometimes a student would persist in submitting insufficient evidence. Others occasionally tried copying someone else's work or claiming their evidence had been lost. In response I continued to maintain high standards for all portfolio entries and encouraged my students to rise to these standards. I also gave extra help to those who were having difficulties. I did not give credit, however, to students whose proofs were blatant copies or to students who lost portfolio materials.

Summary

In this chapter I have shared the kinds of obstacles I had to overcome to institute my program of portfolio assessment. Although I occasionally became frustrated with my approach, student efforts, and time constraints, the overall results were well worth the effort. I have never felt closer to any group of students than to those in my portfolio classes. I came to view my students as individuals through their portfolios. It was exciting for me to implement changes in my classroom that greatly enhanced their opportunities for learning. No longer do I think of leaving the profession.

Portfolio Implementation: Anticipating Challenges

6

Susan Skawinski Lima and Mary Ann Snider are co-directors of the Rhode Island Portfolio Assessment Project. They spent the first two years of the project working with a small group of teachers to develop a model for portfolio implementation. Then they began inviting each of Rhode Island's thirty-seven school districts to send teams of teachers to learn from their model. New teachers join the project each year to develop portfolios and join a network of experienced portfolio teachers who meet regularly to share ideas and solve problems.

Portfolios represent a philosophy of classroom practice that encourages clear expectations, shared decision making, self-reflection, and collaboration. The model of portfolio assessment we have developed is based on four beliefs:

- Good assessment is integrally linked with good instruction and both should focus on student-centered learning.
- The majority of decisions about assessment and instruction should be made by classroom teachers, often in collaboration with students.
- Teachers must establish high expectations for all their students. Portfolios demonstrate and celebrate the unique performances of learners as they progress toward these expectations.

- Parents and families have much to contribute to teachers' understanding of how students learn. Therefore, families should be involved in the development of student portfolios.

The purpose of this chapter is to identify the challenges that emerge and discuss ways to approach each one. Here are four major concerns that teachers raise:
- What goes into a portfolio?
- Where do I find the time to develop and manage portfolios?
- How do I grade and report progress?
- What roles do school and district administrators play in the process?

What Goes into a Portfolio?

The work of the portfolio is to capture snapshots of students' learning about particular content, events, and processes. A collection of these snapshots provides an ongoing history of growth throughout the school year. Portfolio evidence should be directly linked to the learning outcomes established by the teacher (see Chapter 1 for further discussion of this approach to portfolio design).

Learning outcomes are broadly stated expectations of student performance that can be further defined in terms of specific purposes. *Purpose* provides a direct link to instruction and student performances. Moving instruction toward meaningful experiences and discussions that support these purposes can be difficult. In addition, the connections among learning outcomes, purpose, and *evidence* can be ambiguous for many students. It may help to begin the process by focusing on one or two areas of instruction and develop clear instructional purposes for those areas. Then brainstorm a few types of evidence that might "prove" a student has learned these purposes. Finally, plan instructional activities that support the development of student evidence.

For example, let's imagine that one purpose you establish in language arts is to have students understand the basic structure of stories. You might choose story retelling as one of the options students have for giving evidence. You would need to do several things before having your students read and retell a story: First, define what is meant by *retelling*. Second, prepare a model of the content in a retelling. Third, prepare to model the process of creating a retelling. In other words, the features of a retelling (such as identifying relevant details, reflecting the story's organization, and including elements of the story structure) must be identified and used to develop criteria that can be shared with students as part of instruction. Later, these same criteria can be applied by you and your students to assess and improve the retellings.

It is important to avoid the tendency to place almost everything (or very few things) into a portfolio. Here are some guidelines for deciding what belongs:

- Does the portfolio show a student's growth over time? The portfolio might include similar pieces of evidence collected at different points in time over the school year. These pieces can include best work, earlier steps toward a finished product, and even work that shows how the student struggled.

- Does the portfolio contain evidence that addresses growth and development across the curriculum? You can use the portfolio to help students make connections among the subject areas they study.

- Is the evidence varied? The evidence can come in different forms—audiotapes, videotapes, conference notes, photographs, computer disks, or artwork. The evidence can also show how the student works independently and in groups.

- Is each piece in the portfolio accompanied by a clear rationale for its inclusion? The portfolio should show that students are thinking about themselves as learners.

- Does the portfolio give you a sense of the student's interests inside and beyond the classroom? The portfolio can help you understand the "big picture" of the student as a learner.

Where Do I Find the Time to Develop and Manage Portfolios?

Begin slowly and use portfolios as a framework to support the functions of your entire classroom. Portfolios are most overwhelming to teachers whose classrooms are teacher-centered and focused exclusively on covering curriculum. A portfolio classroom is one where teachers shift their focus to establishing an environment where students feel free to take risks while becoming responsible decision makers. As you become comfortable with this new role for your students, you will find time for extended projects, reflection about learning, conferences, student observation, and record keeping.

Establishing a supportive classroom environment is a lofty concept. Here are some practical steps you can take to begin the process:

- Provide clear messages to students that risk taking is encouraged and rewarded.
- Stop grading every piece of student work.
- Invite students to make some decisions about their own learning goals.
- Establish working groups and prepare students to help each other as planners, coaches, and evaluators of work.
- Demonstrate your own thinking and learning for students.
- Decide to let some things go. You can't evaluate everything.

Of course none of this happens quickly or automatically. You will need to commit early parts of the school year to introduce, model, and reinforce these classroom patterns; then extend and modify your plan throughout the year. You will be pleasantly surprised with the abilities of even very young children to become self-directed. Teachers who receive students who have graduated from other portfolio classrooms have an easier time implementing their own portfolios. These students begin the school year prepared to manage their portfolios and direct their own learning.

How Do I Grade and Report Progress?

The information portfolios yield about learners is often inconsistent with traditional expectations for grading and reporting progress. As we struggle with this issue we find it helpful to consider the distinctions between grading and reporting. The purpose of grading is to indicate to students the degree to which their work meets our expectations. The purpose of reporting is to give someone else, usually parents or family members, a summary of student achievement.

Grading

Portfolios are not about grading students but about assessing learning. When you assign grades, you judge performance based on standards you may not discuss in detail with your students (or colleagues). For example, you may be reluctant to give students advance information about a graded test because it may influence how they prepare. As a result, students may be unsure of the reasoning behind the assigned grade.

In contrast, you rate the quality of a piece of portfolio evidence using the same criteria students used to guide the development of their work. Whether they succeed or fail, students must understand the reasoning behind the grades we assign. This mutual understanding sets the teacher up to meet with each student to establish the next steps of learning. In this context, assessment is a tool for planning instruction and facilitating learning as much as it is a tool for grading.

Teachers with little experience in portfolio assessment believe that judgments based on portfolios are largely opinion, whereas traditional grades reflect consistently-applied standards of quality. In fact, the reverse is much more likely to be true. On a number of occasions we have asked teachers to individually grade the same piece of student writing. Without fail, teachers assigned grades that ranged from A's to D's. When asked to justify their decisions, teachers focused on different aspects of the written piece; some teachers were more interested in the conventions of writing, others placed greater value in the expression of ideas, and still others were concerned about coherence.

These kinds of inconsistencies occur less often in portfolio assessment because decisions about instruction and assessment are guided by the same learning outcomes and purposes. The development of these outcomes and purposes requires a classroom consensus about performance and achievement. Specific criteria are established for each piece of portfolio evidence. For example, a teacher's explicit grading criteria for a written narrative might be clarity of expression, organizational coherence, and proper use of mechanics. A proficient piece of evidence would display uniform clarity; consistent coherence; and few errors in spelling, punctuation, and grammar.

Reporting

Report cards are usually structured around single designations of performance such as letter or number grades. Portfolios provide opportunities for rich and detailed descriptions of performance. Ideally, using portfolios leads to a flexible reporting system that allows you to choose the information that best describes student learning and that best meets the needs of learners and families. Options for reporting include cooperative student-parent-teacher conferences, narrative summaries of student progress, and videotapes of you and students working together. The goal is to help parents develop a complete picture of the growth their child has made toward identified learning outcomes and purposes.

What Roles Do School and District Administrators Play in the Process?

Research on instructional change has clearly documented the value of administrative support in developing and sustaining classroom innovations (Leithwood, 1992). Our experience with teachers and schools underscores the critical importance of school-level and district-level administrators understanding and supporting portfolio assessment and the instructional changes such assessment creates.

We have attempted in various ways to encourage administrative participation in portfolio assessment. For example, we ask principals and superintendents to ensure that teachers in the same districts can plan together periodically. We invite administrators to attend our working conferences for portfolio teachers. However, this level of participation does not effectively support sustained portfolio development.

In order to be truly effective, administrators must define their leadership responsibilities in the same language as the teachers' portfolio outcomes. Administrative support for portfolio implementation exists at two levels. The first level occurs when administrators agree to learn and support the specific portfolio goals of teachers. This is an organizational investment because it commits time and energy resources, but it is not a personal investment on the part of the administrator.

The second level of involvement occurs when administrators become actively involved in the development and implementation of portfolios; they attend portfolio development sessions, help establish procedures for implementation, and regularly monitor the effectiveness of the portfolio system. They meet regularly with teachers to contribute to decision making and problem solving. Active administrators tend to be viewed by teachers as allies rather than roadblocks because they make the personal and professional investment necessary to ensure the success of portfolio implementation. Supportive administrators are more typical, but active administrators are more critical to sustained implementation.

Summary of Lessons Learned

Our work in portfolio assessment has taught us many lessons about teaching, learning, instruction, and assessment:

1. Clear goals for student learning play a critical role in linking instruction and assessment. The heart of portfolio assessment is the set of high expectations you develop to guide your students' learning, and these expectations form the basis for each instructional decision you make. Learning goals then become the context for assessment activities— you and students choose pieces of evidence that exemplify learning goals. The process that results is a continuous circle of learning goals informing instructional decisions and linked to assessment planning.

2. Teachers need a supportive network through which they can test ideas, solve problems, identify alternative approaches, and share successes. Using these uninterrupted blocks of time, teachers in our project are able to reach agreement about learner outcomes, develop criteria, discuss potential pieces of evidence, and share benchmarks of student performance. They identify these opportunities as the most critical element in the success of the project.

3. Administrative involvement has a significant influence on the effectiveness of portfolio implementation. The greater the active engagement of administrators, particularly principals, the greater the success of portfolio practice.

Knowledgeable administrators can support classroom implementation with necessary resources, and they can facilitate broad-based discussions about student learning outcomes, purposes, and evidence criteria. These administrators can modify existing administrative practices (such as reporting systems) to accommodate portfolio design. They can also encourage other teachers and administrators to become involved in portfolio assessment.

4. Parents who understand portfolio assessment are our most important advocates. Portfolios are meaningful to parents because they offer more information than letter grades and help to show a child's growth over time. And, although many parents are not ready to surrender report cards, most are prepared to become powerful allies for portfolios. They, along with their children, want concrete standards of performance.

5. We must take risks when undergoing change. Begin slowly; we find that the most successful approach is to build a portfolio system over a period of several years as you become more experienced and comfortable with the components of the process.

Using Portfolios to Assess
Your Own Instruction

7

*Susan Pasquarelli is an assistant professor of education
at Roger Williams University in Bristol, Rhode Island. In
this chapter she shares her experiences using portfolios to
help you consider and improve your instructional practices.*

Introduction

"How do I know if I'm meeting all of my students' specific
needs during instruction?" asked one experienced teacher on
the first night of our graduate seminar on teaching language
arts. It was a question I hoped to answer by having my students
keep portfolios of their instructional plans and materials. I knew
that other teachers report that portfolios can yield far more
information for both the teacher and the student than traditional
testing measures (Paris, 1991).

A portfolio approach to assessment includes a wide variety
of student work. It also supports teacher-student collaboration
and an emphasis on examining learning processes (Tierney,
Carter, and Desai, 1991). These guiding principles proved to be
very helpful to my particular community of learners. We discovered together that portfolios demand meaningful interactions
with everyone in the classroom. Our constant collaboration and
"teacher talk" provided us with detailed knowledge about our-

selves as teachers. This practice is also supported by Bandura and Wood (1989), who identify self-assessment as one of the most effective processes for making judgments about one's own competence.

Developing Portfolios to Highlight Instructional Practices

The portfolio I developed consisted of three interacting components: setting explicit purposes, creating specific evidence to indicate attainment of these purposes, and articulating clear assessment criteria to evaluate the evidence (see Chapter 1 in this same volume for a detailed description of this portfolio design). I based my instructional goals on the professional needs of my students, who were elementary teachers studying to become reading specialists. I chose three purposes for my students and asked each of them to determine an additional purpose for himself or herself. Next I selected a variety of evidence options, again leaving some room for student choice. My students' motivation for instructional planning was high in this learning environment. They were able to visualize their own students as they set their purposes and designed instructional evidence for me.

The assessment criteria I used to determine the strengths and needs of my students' evidence were designed to reflect current thinking on literacy instruction. For example, when my students submitted a lesson plan as evidence, they knew in advance what instructional methods should be included to support their students' participation in the lesson.

As my students developed their individual portfolios, they were asked to provide a written caption for each piece of evidence they submitted. To this end, I provided them with frequent opportunities to conference and share their evidence with peers. We found ourselves collaborating on the entire process of portfolio development as the semester progressed.

Around midsemester, I realized we were harvesting far more from our portfolios than I had originally anticipated. The portfolios had provided my class with a forum for ongoing assessment of ourselves as teachers.

Self-Assessment

My students assessed themselves in a variety of ways while developing their portfolios.

Captioning evidence

My students wrote captions that identified each piece of evidence, explained its purpose, and commented on its quality. I asked them to provide captions while the evidence was being developed *and* when the evidence was completed. Wolf (1989) describes this self-reflective process as an opportunity for students to tell a story full of words such as *then, before, later,* and *now,* especially if students include and reflect upon more than one version of their evidence. My students found it worthwhile to go back to their earlier drafts to find benchmarks of improvement. At the end of the course I had each student share a story about the evolution of one piece of evidence. This technique confirmed their own sense of growth as teachers. As one student said:

> *I'm recognizing things that I didn't recognize before. You know, ways that we really hurt kids in the classroom. For example, I go up in front of them with too many ideas and no real purpose. When you know you have a weakness in a certain area, you self-assess especially for that.*

Reflective journals

Described by Atwell (1990), a learning log is a written record in which students make plans, record observations, integrate new information with prior knowledge, and make self-reflections and elaborations. My students reported that keeping a journal increased their abilities to systematically assess their lesson plans before and after conducting a lesson. We used a variety of formats in this journal.

One of the students in my course used her journal as a record-keeping device for the literacy instruction she implemented in her own classroom. She reported an increased awareness of her own strengths and needs in both planning and revising instructional procedures. She also reported a greater ability to reach those students who traditionally "got lost" during instruction. Her comments in relation to this benefit of keeping a journal were:

> *I can't believe how much better I am at reaching my students who have had trouble in the past. Could it be that their success is due to my spending more time deliberately planning and revising for their instruction?*

Verbal self-reports

To self-report, my students thought-aloud (Hayes and Flower, 1980) about the processes they used to accomplish a task. One important student payoff for this effort was an increased ability to identify previously unseen flaws in their instructional plans. In the following example, I use the think-aloud process with a student to check his understanding of a lesson:

Teacher: *What constitutes a cohesive lesson?*

Student: *When I go through and it makes sense and it follows step by step and there is nothing missing.*

Teacher: *How do you determine there's something missing?*

Student: *I play it in my mind. You know, I'm reading it aloud and then I stop and think aloud after each section. It helps me to answer these questions: Does it make sense? Do the students need to know anything else to use this strategy? Could students in third grade do this after this amount of instruction? What is missing?*

Peer interaction

My students were continually in need of teacher and peer support to make sense of what they were learning in my course. Tanner-Cazinha et al. (1991) state, "Dialogue can bring teachers and students together to achieve a shared understanding of evaluation that will assist . . . students." The following is a student's report about how peer interactions aided in self-assessment:

> *When I read my rough draft of my lesson to another teacher, and I looked at what I had planned, I said, well this is OK, but let's take it a step further and let's make it clearer so that I could put this onto a poster or I could draw it on the board in this model so the kids could see it in a more clarified form. I didn't notice the lack of specificity of the lesson before I worked with the other teacher.*

As an added benefit many of my students reported teaching these same self-assessment methods to their own students to help them develop as readers and writers.

How Portfolios Influence Instruction

My students gained an impressive amount of knowledge about instructional language and flexible literacy practices as they developed their portfolios. They also reported a deeper understanding of the importance of monitoring their own instruction in the future. I noted with particular satisfaction the confidence they gained about their own competence as they learned to talk about literacy instruction.

One student articulated ways of modeling that worked for her students:

*In my instructional plan, I modeled two ways: a good
way and a way that showed a lot of things that needed
improvement. And the students were able to see the differences; they could pull out things that were good techniques and things that were not good. From there, we
identified the steps in the use of a speaking strategy. I feel
that this will be a highly effective instructional technique
for all students.*

Another student demonstrated her ability to articulate clear
instructional plans (and it is interesting to note that she builds
student self-assessment into her lesson):

*. . . the students are going to record their oral reading
on an audiotape for independent practice, then they will
work in pairs to analyze each other's oral reading and
discuss the problems they have, and then fill out a check-
list for voice control. Then they will share with the class
any problems they had with the strategy and how they
could monitor them. I chose self-assessment for them
because they need to monitor for this speaking skill—
they shouldn't rely on their audience; they should be
actively thinking about their own voice control as they
are reading aloud.*

During a discussion about purpose setting, another student
related this strategy for lesson planning:

*I try to plan a lesson that has a strong purpose. So, in a
new lesson, I want to draw back into that. If you don't
keep reinforcing that lesson from the past the kids won't
draw upon it again.*

At the end of the course, my students offered overwhelmingly positive responses to the question, "How did using portfolios influence you instructionally?" The following is a representative selection of these responses:

- *It forced me to take a systematized look at my instructional plans.*
- *It encouraged me to collaborate and conference with able peers and other professionals to identify my strengths and needs.*
- *It led me to a greater awareness of what I am doing well and what I am not doing well.*
- *It provided me with ways to assess each new instructional approach I try.*
- *It encouraged me to change or revise some of my current instructional practices.*

Conclusion

The portfolio development process described herein took place over one semester in a teacher education course. My students reported that the benefits of using portfolios far outweighed the time and hard work it took to develop them. They came to believe that effective literacy instruction for a diverse student body requires a quality of thinking that only structured self-assessment can produce.

Although knowledge about theoretically sound assessment practices was a primary contributor to the portfolios we created, many of the portfolio features I've described were the result of trial and error. Along the way I learned one additional piece of information about teacher developed portfolios: many of the best components evolve as a result of pure discovery. I hope this advice and the student experiences I've described in this chapter help you to consider ways of using the portfolios you develop to assess and refine your own instructional practices.

The Promise and Challenges of Educational Portfolios: Themes from the Book Chapters

8

Steven Z. Athanases is acting assistant professor of education at Stanford University. He directs a project researching ways to assess progressive instruction built around communities of learners. Steven used portfolios in his teaching of high school English, worked with elementary school teachers to design portfolios of integrated language arts instruction for the Teacher Assessment Project at Stanford, and consulted for the National Board for Professional Teaching Standards on development and evaluation of teacher portfolios and other alternative assessments.

Lessons from the Book: An Introduction

Quality of assessment often lags behind innovations in curriculum and instruction. Often we will see progressive classroom instruction and enhanced student learning evaluated in ways that simply don't match the classroom realities—ways that fail to measure the complexity of what has occurred. Among the methods of assessment educators and policy makers have explored in recent years to close the gap between instruction and evaluation is the educational portfolio. Education conferences and recent publications frequently feature the portfolio. The diverse group of educators whose work is represented in this book add their voices to this chorus. Although the authors in this book may have begun with the goal of strengthening assessment procedures and engaging students in the process of assessment, they report a range of benefits of classroom portfolio use, many of which move beyond assessment per se. This is the key lesson from this book.

A second lesson is that portfolios apparently can serve valuable functions in an enormous range of educational settings. The chapters describe the use of portfolios in twelve different contexts; eleven of these are classrooms and the twelfth is a professional development program for in-service teachers. The reports come from a variety of geographic locations—from rural Florida to a bilingual classroom on the outskirts of El Paso to a university in the Pacific Northwest. The grade levels range from kindergarten through middle school and high school and on to classes for master's students in teacher-education programs and workshops for practicing teachers. The subject matters in which portfolios were explored are likewise varied, covering math, chemistry, language arts, social studies, curriculum instruction, literacy, and science. Finally, the school environments varied in the amount of on-site support the teachers received for their portfolio experimentation, from a school in which administrators fostered change to one with a highly rigid evaluation program in which the teacher worked alone to implement portfolios. Despite these differences in region, grade level, subject matter, and available support, the stories of portfolio experimentation share a number of themes and concerns that this chapter highlights.

Any significant change in curriculum, instruction, or assessment requires a great deal of teacher time and, as these chapters attest, explorations into the use of classroom portfolios is no exception. Why, then, should anyone bother? Most of the reports identify, explicitly or implicitly, the goal of developing a mode of assessment that is more effective than traditional tests—one that captures the learning students do and the growth they make over time and one that engages students in the processes of documenting and evaluating their work. The reports describe how portfolios meet these objectives through their collections of documents and other captioned items to provide evidence over time of student learning toward prespecified goals.

This chapter begins by highlighting two common features of the portfolios described in this book, followed by authors' suggestions for effectively implementing the portfolio process. This chapter continues with teachers' reports of the values of implementing portfolios and concludes with some suggestions for further exploration and study.

Common Features of the Portfolios

Chapter 1 lays out a portfolio design that James Barton and Angelo Collins illustrate with their experiences with preservice teachers in reading/literacy and in science. Two of the elements of their design are reinforced so thoroughly by various other authors in the volume that they warrant brief discussion.

Explicitness of purpose and goals

James and Angelo ground portfolio documentation in clear purposes and learning goals. In this way, documentation is selective and the portfolio does not become an overwhelmingly large container with all but the kitchen sink included. The authors in this book vary in the degree of ownership they offer students in identifying learning goals, but they agree on the importance of being selective about goals and about the centrality of goals in the documentation process. Suzanne Weiner notes the importance of teachers and students learning to think of documents as evidence tied tightly to goals. Susan Butler describes how her high school students needed to learn that they must prove their learning in relation to unit goals by supplying ample evidence. To emphasize the centrality of learning goals in the portfolio process, Angie Williams reports how she learned to specify unit goals at the outset and learned the importance of posting these goals on large signs above the blackboard in her classroom.

Multiple sources for documentation

When students offer evidence of their learning through varied forms of documentation, they create more convincing proof that they have met the course goals. You, as the teacher, can see how different kinds of information converge on similar results. The authors suggest many possible documents that can be included in portfolios to serve as evidence of learning including: audiotapes, videotapes, excerpts from learning logs or journals, notes from teacher observations, attestations of learning from other individuals, relevant out-of-school sources providing evidence of learning occurring off school grounds, photographs, homework, outlines, worksheets, review sheets, tests, lab reports, and collaborative write-ups.

Dorla Long provides a particularly extensive list of possible documents she invited her fourth and fifth graders to use in their portfolios of language arts learning. Beyond documents already named, she suggests including class magazines, dioramas, photographs, book reports, special-interest reports, drawings, models, booklets, interviews, and projects. Preservice teachers in James Barton's class included graphic illustrations of lessons, and those in Angelo Collins' class included videotapes of their teaching. Many of the chapter authors ask students for captions that clearly identify the document and, in some cases, explain how the document serves as evidence of learning related to a course goal. In addition, student reflections hold an important place in the portfolio as students review their work and explore the degree to which it serves as evidence of having attained learning goals.

Implementation Suggestions

The authors in this book draw on their experiences to suggest ways to make the portfolio process go smoothly. Based on their work with Rhode Island teachers implementing classroom portfolios, Susan Skawinski Lima and Mary Ann Snider urge a gradual introduction of the process over a period of three years. Various authors suggest that students need scaffolding, or learning supports, in order to move successfully to a portfolio process. Angie Williams found the process smoother when she wrote a letter to her students that detailed instructions before she started a unit with portfolio documentation. She also posted the unit goals above the blackboard to anchor her students' work. Angie used in-class time for portfolio assembly so that students could examine their work and create additional evidence if necessary. Finally, she notes the importance of keeping parents and students informed of portfolio due dates and of holding periodic in-class portfolio workshops. In still other classes, the authors structured class time for students to review and critique each other's portfolios and to work collaboratively to generate criteria for portfolio evaluation. For some students, constructing scoring criteria enabled them to better meet portfolio expectations.

In her work with teacher education students, Suzanne Weiner asked students to write about and discuss the portfolio learning process. She found that students needed support in understanding relevant vocabulary and in moving beyond jargon. One of her students suggested that a model portfolio would help students understand what such a new concept can look like in real form. In fact, various portfolio development groups have found the need to provide a range of examples of the forms portfolios can take. You might want to collect various examples to show future students the possibilities of portfolios. If you show students multiple and very different examples, students may open up to new possibilities and see how different routes can lead to similar goals.

Finally, a few authors in this book suggest that the process of implementing portfolios can go much more smoothly when other key adults get involved. Susan Skawinski Lima and Mary Ann Snider stress the critical importance of school-level and district-level support for the process. They likewise suggest involving parents in the process so that they become advocates rather than potential critics of the reform initiative. Other authors identify the value of working collaboratively with other teachers to sort through the challenging process of introducing classroom portfolios, perhaps at multiple grade levels in a single school to build a sense of continuity and to develop a portfolio "culture" within a school.

Reports of the Values of Classroom Portfolio Use

The authors reported a range of values from having introduced portfolios in their classrooms. One key value was that portfolios served students as a formative evaluation tool; that is, students learned through portfolio use how various areas of their learning had progressed and where they needed to increase their attention. The portfolio provided performance snapshots at various checkpoints along the way and provided students with some information about how to grow. These are no small achievements for classrooms. Some of the authors reported that portfolios were also formative evaluation tools for them as teachers, informing them, at times, of learning goals that very few students reached—areas that perhaps needed increased instructional time and care. In response to such information, some of the authors reported sharpening their goals and their instruction.

The authors identified three areas of student learning most affected by portfolio use. First, students learned to take ownership of the process of documenting their learning. In this way, they learned to be authors of their portfolios, responsible for telling the story as fully as they could. Second, some students apparently learned through the portfolio process how to be more reflective about their own learning and achievement. Students were gaining a sense of awareness of themselves as learners. This kind of awareness can serve as a learner's stepping stone to greater self-regulation of learning. Third, some authors reported that their students learned things not only about understanding their own learning but also about assessing it.

At its best, the portfolio implementation became a highly engaging and learning-rich process. Angie Williams provides a compelling report of how she used the successes and problems of portfolio implementation during a five-week unit on genetics to revise the process for a second five-week unit on the circulatory system. By providing students with in-class time to assemble their portfolios, they were able to learn about holes in their documentation, goals they could not clearly claim to have achieved. Angie describes the pleasure of watching students create pieces of evidence that no teacher had assigned—"work of their own design." These "second chances for learning" during unit-culminating portfolio assembly clarified to students how the portfolio process allowed for continuing opportunities to increase the quality of their work. Angie notes, "There was still time to succeed if they realized they had not adequately learned something or had no evidence to prove it." The engagement Angie reports seeing in her sixth graders as they worked through the portfolio process is not unlike what Susan Butler reported seeing in her tenth-grade chemistry students (some of whom renewed interest in school) and in herself (she tells us the challenge and renewal of the process may have kept her in the profession).

Just as the artist's portfolio can stimulate conversation about an artist's work, the classroom portfolio, according to a number of the authors in this book, served as a stimulus for communication in some important ways. One author reports that students engaged in productive talk as they reviewed and critiqued one another's portfolios. A number of the authors found they had far better documentation of student learning to use as a foundation for communicating with their students about goals and progress. An important piece of that communication is the links among parents, children, and teachers that the portfolio process can foster. Jeannie Clarkson, for example, reports that parents were able to see their children's growth over time and, when viewing their children's portfolios periodically, were able to become partners in their children's education rather than the last ones to know what their children are up to, a common complaint among parents. Dorla Long invited parents to give responses to student work, insights on student learning, and feedback on the process. She offers a quotation from the mother of Meg, a special-needs child, who says that discussion between Meg and her teacher about score discrepancies in evaluation of the portfolio was a good motivator for Meg, as she tended to score herself higher than a reader might. This kind of parent input can be invaluable for a teacher and ultimately for a student's learning.

Suggestions for Further Exploration and Study

The chapters in this book suggest some areas that you, along with other researchers and educators, might study in order to advance the work on portfolios.

Suggestions for development in documentation

In her work on teacher science portfolios, Angelo says the best portfolios have included a student's clear purpose statement, a "road map through the evidence," and an insightful final reflective statement. All three of these documents (purpose statement, road map, and reflective statement) sound promising for use in a range of settings. What do these look like? What kinds of guidelines do students receive for constructing such documents? Susan Pasquarelli suggests that captions on portfolio documents can be powerful indicators of learning and that her students search their work for "benchmarks of improvement." Again, these sound like promising documents and activities that warrant more discussion. Purpose statements, captions, road maps through evidence, and reflective statements can serve as vital tools for communicating to others what one has learned.

These are some of the more elusive elements of the portfolio that we need to understand better so we can help our students learn to use these tools. Illustrations of these documents, showing what they reveal to teachers and other portfolio reviewers about student learning and how they shape reviewers' responses to portfolios, can help advance the work on portfolios.

Documentation and analysis of evaluation and scoring

Two problems of evaluating and scoring portfolios surfaced in the reports in this book: (1) How should portfolios be evaluated? and (2) How can the evaluation process be made efficient? These are two problems that constantly arise in development work on alternative assessments. In determining effective evaluation procedures, clear evaluation criteria need to be identified, and some care needs to be given to reliability of scoring (whether various reviewers using the same criteria will arrive at similar evaluations of the same portfolio). Susan Skawinski Lima and Mary Ann Snider argue that a group of teachers can address the problem of subjectivity by identifying criteria for assessing how well evidence satisfies goals. Dorla Long states she and her students do independent ratings of student portfolios and then compare their ratings. In this way, she works toward some reliability in scoring, using clear evaluation criteria as a guide.

Future exploration of portfolios would be more complete with some detailed case studies of how different reviewers used similar scoring criteria to evaluate student work. This would help with the difficult process of moving from grading individual pieces of student work to the new challenge of looking across various documents or pieces of evidence to see how well learning goals have been satisfied. In addition, some educators may value seeing what two or three different sets of scoring criteria might yield in the review of single student portfolios.

Finally, this book's authors are nearly unanimous in asserting that portfolio review requires a great deal of time. This concern suggests that many teachers would value the development of inventive ways to review and evaluate portfolios that do not tax teachers to the limit. Angie Williams calls for an evaluation form that would communicate much information but require little teacher writing. Others would prefer note-taking that could yield brief reports. Whatever forms are developed, educators appear hungry for creative tools to streamline the review and evaluation process.

Research on the impact of portfolios

Much of the work on the use of portfolios proposes things to try or provides accounts of what teachers have tried. Little work has given us detailed examinations of what occurs in classrooms where portfolios have been used. This book suggests areas that you might want to investigate in order to help the larger educational community better understand what portfolios can yield. First, some of the authors in this book suggest ways to use portfolios to engage parents in their children's learning process. Keeping records of how parents become engaged could reveal the value of linking classroom learning with the outside community. Second, some of the authors suggest that the power of the portfolio is as much a function of the learning processes associated with assembling and reviewing the portfolio as it is a function of the portfolio as an evaluation product.

What do students do in their peer portfolio conferences? What do the student voices sound like as they make sense of their own and their peers' documents and as they try to caption these documents for use as evidence? Finally, how does the portfolio process affect students' learning, their self-esteem, and their understanding of learning and assessment? Detailed documentation of the process, again with particular attention to student work and student voices, might shed more light on the promise of classroom portfolios that this book has suggested.

References

Atwell, N. *Coming to Know: Writing to Learn in the Middle Grades.* Portsmouth, N.H.: Heinemann, 1990.

Bandura, A., and R. Wood. "Effect of Perceived Controllability Making." *Journal of Personality and Social Psychology,* Vol. 45 (1989), pp. 1017–1028.

Bird, T. "The Schoolteacher's Portfolio: An Essay on Possibilities," *Handbook of Teacher Evaluation: Elementary and Secondary Personnel,* 2nd ed., eds. J. Millman and L. Darling-Hammond. Newbury Park, Calif.: Sage, 1990.

Collins, A. "Portfolios for Biology Teacher Assessment." *Journal of Personnel Evaluation in Education,* Vol. 5 (1991), pp. 147–167.

Collins, A. "Portfolios: Questions for Design." *Science Scope* (March 1992), pp. 25–27.

Elbow, P. Foreword to *Portfolios: Process and Product,* eds. P. Belanoff and M. Dickson. Portsmouth, N.H.: Boynton/Cook, 1991.

Florida Department of Education. "Course Student Performance Standards, Chemistry I Honors." *Curriculum Framework.* Tallahassee, Fla.: Department of Education, 1991.

Graves, D. H., and B. S. Sunstein, eds. *Portfolio Portraits.* Portsmouth, N.H.: Heinemann, 1992.

Haertel, E. "From Expert Opinions to Reliable Scores: Psychometrics for Judgment-Based Teacher Assessment." Paper presented at the annual meeting of the American Educational Research Association, Boston, 1990.

Hayes, J., and L. Flower. "Identifying the Organization of Writing Processes," *Cognitive Processes in Writing,* eds. L. Gregg and E. Steinberg. Hillsdale, N.J.: Lawrence Earlbaum Assoc., 1980.

Leithwood, K. A. "The Move Toward Transformational Leadership." *Educational Leadership*, Vol. 49, No. 5 (1992), pp. 8–12.

Ott, J. "Performance Assessment," *Merrill Algebra I.* New York: Macmillan/McGraw Hill, 1993.

Paris, S. G. "Portfolio Assessment of Young Readers." *The Reading Teacher,* Vol. 44, No. 9 (1991), pp. 680–681.

Paulson, L., and P. Paulson. "How Do Portfolios Measure Up? A Cognitive Model for Assessing Portfolios." ERIC Documents. Paper presented at the "Aggregating Portfolio Data" conference sponsored by the Northwest Evaluation Association, Union, Wash., 1990.

Tanner-Cazinha, D., K. Au, and K. Blake. "New Perspectives on Literacy Evaluation." *Language Arts,* Vol. 68, No. 8 (1991), pp. 669–673.

Tierney, R. J., M. A. Carter, and L. E. Desai. *Portfolio Assessment in the Reading-Writing Classroom.* Norwood, Mass.: Christopher Gordon Publishers, 1991.

Tobin, K., J. B. Kahle, and B. J. Fraser, eds. *Windows into Science Classrooms.* New York: The Falmer Press, 1990.

Valencia, S. W., W. McGinley, and P. D. Pearson. *Assessing Reading and Writing: Building a More Complete Picture for Middle School Assessment.* Center for the Study of Reading, Technical Report 500. Urbana, Ill.: 1990.

Valencia, S. W., E. H. Hiebert, and P. P. Afflerbach, eds. *Authentic Reading Assessment: Practices and Possibilities*. Newark, Del.: International Reading Association, 1994.

Valencia, S. W., and N. A. Place. "Literacy Portfolios for Teaching, Learning, and Accountability: The Bellevue Literacy Assessment Project," *Authentic Reading Assessment: Practices and Possibilities,* eds. S. W. Valencia, E. H. Hiebert, and P. P. Afflerbach. Newark, Del.: International Reading Association, 1994.

Wiggins, G. "A True Test: Toward More Authentic and Equitable Assessment." *Phi Delta Kappan* (1989), pp. 703–713.

Winograd, P., S. Paris, and C. Bridge. "Improving the Assessment of Literacy." *The Reading Teacher,* Vol. 45 (2) (1991), pp. 108–116.

Wolf, D. "Portfolio Assessment: Sampling Student Work." *Educational Leadership,* Vol. 46, No. 7 (1989), pp. 4–10.